DIEPPE –
August 19th 1942

The lucky few who survived the bloody inferno of Dieppe arrived back in their home ports battered, bewildered and, most of all, angry. They had left behind more than two-thirds of their original number – either dead or taken prisoner by the Germans.

Why? What went wrong? Were the Germans forewarned of the attack – did the encounter with the enemy alert the shore defences? Or was the whole affair a colossal military blunder – a staged sacrificial attack forced on Britain by her Allies?

Eric Maguire has analysed the operation from its conception to its final tragic conclusion, and throws new light upon this most dramatic and fatal episode. Here is the authentic story of the battle as it appeared to the men who fought it – British, Canadian and German – and to the French people living in and around Dieppe who were so rudely awakened on that terrible morning . . .

Eric Maguire

Dieppe
August 19th 1942

CORGI BOOKS
A DIVISION OF TRANSWORLD PUBLISHERS LTD

DIEPPE AUGUST 19th 1942

A CORGI BOOK 0 552 09575 3

Originally published in Great Britain
by Jonathan Cape Ltd.

PRINTING HISTORY
Jonathan Cape edition published 1963
Corgi edition published 1974

Copyright © 1963 by Eric Maguire

This book is set in 10pt. Baskerville

Corgi Books are published by
Transworld Publishers Ltd.,
Cavendish House, 57–59 Uxbridge Road,
Ealing, London W.5.
Made and printed in Great Britain by
Cox & Wyman Ltd., London, Reading and Fakenham

CONTENTS

ILLUSTRATIONS

Between pages 96 and 97

Dieppe. Low-level photograph (*Reproduced by permission of the Imperial War Museum, London*)

Some of No. 4 Commandos landing at Vasterival (*Reproduced by permission of the Imperial War Museum, London*)

Landing-craft approaching the beach (*Keystone Press Agency Ltd., London*)

Disabled Canadian tank (*Keystone Press Agency Ltd., London*)

Lord Lovat and Commandos after Dieppe (*Reproduced by permission of the Imperial War Museum, London*)

After the battle. Canadian wounded being tended by their comrades (*Keystone Press Agency Ltd., London*)

Commandos disembarking at Newhaven (*Reproduced by permission of the Imperial War Museum, London*)

Aftermath, White Beach (*Reproduced by permission of the Imperial War Museum, London*)

ACKNOWLEDGMENTS

I wish to thank the officials of the Bundesarchiv at Coblenz, Germany, for their courtesy in making available a copy of the war diary of the German 302nd Division. I am also most grateful to Monsieur Georges Guibon of Dieppe for a copy of his diary.

I thank all the Canadian and British veterans of the battle who sent me their personal stories of the day, especially Brigadier Derek Mills-Roberts and Captain R. Wills for their invaluable help in reconstructing the Commando actions.

Above all, I am deeply indebted to Brigadier Peter Young for his patience in reading my draft typescript and for his helpful comments thereon.

At this point I must state that all opinions and comments in this book are strictly my own, and are not in any way the views of any of the individuals whose names are mentioned in the narrative. These people are referred to by the rank they held at the time of action.

ERIC MAGUIRE

Dublin
April, 1963

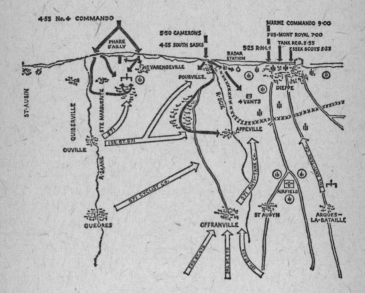

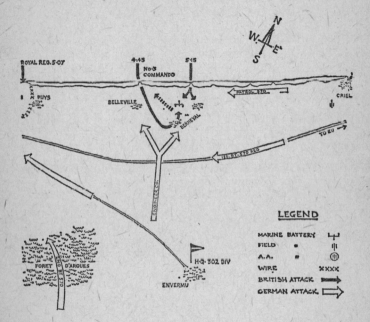

ROYAL REG. 5·07

4·45   5·15

No·3 COMMANDO

PATROL 570

PUYS

BELLEVILLE

BEAUVAL

CRIEL

FRENCH 570 REG.

TO EU

ENGINEER CO.

FORET D'ARQUES

H·Q· 302 DIV

ENVERMU

N
W   E
S

LEGEND

MARINE BATTERY	Ⴑ
FIELD	●	屮
A.A.	◪	⊕
WIRE	XXXX
BRITISH ATTACK	➤➤➤
GERMAN ATTACK	⬜⟩

Preface

THIS is the story of the Dieppe Raid – the story of the blackest day in Canadian military history – a day in which the Canadian Army lost more men as prisoners of war than they did in all the rest of the European campaign.

Especially is it the saga of the 2nd Canadian Division, mettlesome troops who, though highly trained, had never heard a shot fired in anger until the fatal morning of 19th August when they were unloaded on the beaches of Dieppe and Puys, lacking both bombardment and surprise, to face a well-entrenched and alert enemy.

This is the story of a disaster which later was to be presented to the world as a contribution of the utmost value to the future conduct of the war – a disaster brought about by an assault plan which was described by the Germans as an excellent map exercise, and as such did not allow for enemy interference in its execution.

Here, too, is the story of the events which were to culminate in seven long and fear-filled hours on the smoke-shrouded beaches, where disciplined formations were, in a few minutes, reduced to scattered groups of badly shocked individuals, blind and deaf to all but the primeval need of survival. This is the story of men whose world had of a sudden shrunk to a few feet of hard stones – men who found themselves prisoners in a fiendish web of noise and death, from which there seemed no escape.

Is it any wonder that many of those who lived through the inferno will not, even now, talk about it? Those who do talk tell much the same story. 'We came ashore under a terrible fire – men were falling all around – we took whatever cover we could find and waited. We were dismayed because we had not expected anything like this.'

They waited: waited for the orders that never came,

because the men who could give them were either dead or were also waiting for orders. From junior officers to Company commanders, to Battalion commanders, to Brigadiers, to Force Commander, the chain of command was reduced to a state of paralysis.

Some of the later arrivals, their vessels battered and smashed before they reached land, quailed at the sight of the smoking, corpse-strewn beach, and were reluctant to leave the false security of their ships. Can anyone find it in his heart to blame them?

Yet, when the first shattering shock had passed, discipline and courage took over once again, and out of the horror and desolation of the beach arose men of resolution – men who knew what they had to do and did it, fighting back savagely, storming into the town with a fierce desire to get to grips with their invisible enemy. Here is the story of the Commando attacks on the enemy marine batteries covering the sea approaches to Dieppe – that on the right flank a brilliant success, and that on the left a no less brilliant failure.

This, then, is the story of an excursion to Dieppe, and of the men who made it. To these men – to the Royal Navy who carried them and to the R.A.F. who protected them, to the German 302nd Division who were waiting for them, to all who fought and suffered at Dieppe – I dedicate this book.

Anticipation

To the citizens of Dieppe Tuesday, 18th August, 1942, had no special significance. It was just another warm day in the third summer of the occupation, notable perhaps because the news of a devasting air-raid on Rouen was circulating, but otherwise no different from any other day. Life in a town situated as was Dieppe, only seventy miles from England and literally in the front line, was, of course, subject to peculiar hazards and uncertainties, but the population had succeeded in adapting themselves to the conditions and restrictions reasonably well.

The beaches and cliff tops were out of bounds, which meant no bathing or picnics during the fine weather, and as the Casino had been fortified by the Germans there were no little games of *boule* or baccarat to while away the evenings. But things could have been worse – apart from occasional small-scale air raids on German positions around the town, the war had not touched them since June 1940, when the British were withdrawing from France and there had been heavy fighting in the countryside as the Highland Division retreated for their last stand at St. Valéry farther down the coast.

Existence for the past two years had been drab and depressing, with rationing, shortages and queues ever-present features in the daily round, but for the past few weeks a distinct tension was perceptible in the air. It had not passed without notice that the Germans were busy strengthening the beach defences – laying down more wire, putting down additional minefields on the cliffs – and a few days ago they had blown up the west wing of the Casino, much to the detriment of the windows in the adjoining streets. There was much talk of a second front, and it was known that rumours of Allied landings on various parts of the coast were rife amongst the Occupying forces. The Germans were evidently uneasy and seemed to be in a constant state of alert. People had observed portable tank-traps and mobile guns being brought on to the sea front during the night and removed just before dawn. Something seemed to be in the wind, but in spite of all these preparations French opinion, in general, considered that the time was not yet ripe for invasion. This somewhat complacent attitude received a jolt when on the 18th it was made known that several railway stations between Dieppe and Rouen had been bombed, and when later the radio announced that Mr Churchill had been to Moscow, people began to wonder. However, they had had scares before, and their attitude was, in the main, one of fatalism. Very few really believed that the signs and portents meant anything, and they went about their business and made their plans for the morrow as they had always done, war or no war.

Monsieur and Madame P. prepared for a trip to Paris by the early morning train; Madame T. set aside fruit for jam which she would make the next day; Dr. M., who lived in the Rue de Sygogne, arranged to operate on a patient in the Central Hospital at eight o'clock the following morning.

During the afternoon there was an alarm and some anti-aircraft fire from the outskirts of the town. A small British plane travelling very fast and low appeared from the east, flew along the beach and vanished in the sea haze. Such incidents were common and nobody took much notice or bothered to go to the shelters.

As the day drew to a close the streets emptied and black-out curtains were in evidence. Owing to the curfew the town went to bed early, and by nightfall everywhere was silent and deserted.

To the German Command 18th August was of some importance, marking as it did the end of the alert period. Early in the morning of the 19th, for the last time that summer, high tide would coincide with the last hour of darkness, a condition considered essential to any sea-borne attack. If nothing happened then, there was little likelihood of any invasion until the following year.

Since the beginning of July, the troops in the Dieppe area had been in the highest state of readiness, and all ranks were thoroughly bored with the whole business and tired of the constant drilling and training which had proceeded at fever pitch during the past few months. A great deal of work had been done improving and adding to the fortifications in and around the town, and work was still in progress.

To the rank and file of German troops these preparations seemed ominous and, when linked with the wild stories circulating, could mean only one thing – that an invasion was likely.

At this time Dieppe was garrisoned by the 571st Regiment of the 302nd Division, not by any standards first-class combat troops but considered good enough for the job of coastal defence. There were many middle-aged soldiers amongst them and only two days previously a large number of the rawest recruits had been drafted in. Stiffened by a large number of N.C.O.s, these troops would bear the brunt of any invasion attempt, while the crack forces, farther back were deploying into position. Not surprisingly they were nervous, and 'Der Tommy kommt' was on everyone's lips. He might come from the sea or from the sky, or from both directions at once – who could tell?

An Order of the Day from the Commander of the 15th Army dated August did nothing to reassure them. This read:

ORDER OF THE DAY

G.O.C. 15*th Army*   *Army H.Q.* 10–8–42.

The information in our hands makes it clear that the Anglo-Americans will be forced, in spite of themselves, by the wretched predicament of the Russians, to undertake some operation in the West in the near future. They must do something

    (a) in order to keep their Russian allies fighting;
    (b) for home front reasons.

I have repeatedly brought this to the attention of the troops and I ask that my orders on this matter be kept constantly before them so that the idea sinks in thoroughly and they expect henceforward nothing else. The troops must grasp the fact that when it happens it will be a very sticky business.

Bombing and strafing from the air, shelling from the sea, commandos and assault boats, parachutists and air-landing troops, hostile civilians, sabotage and murder – all these they will have to face with steady nerves if they are not to go under. On no account must the troops let themselves get rattled. Fear is not to be thought of. When the muck begins to fly the troops must wipe their eyes and ears, grip their weapons more tightly and fight as they have never fought before.

THEM OR US

that must be the watchword for each man.

The Führer has given the German Armed Forces tasks of every kind in the past and all have been carried out. The task which now confronts us will also be carried out. My men will not prove the worst. I have looked into your eyes. I know you are German men.

You will gladly do your simple duty to the death.
Do this and you will remain victorious.

Long live our People and our Fatherland.
Long live our Führer ADOLF HITLER.

Your Commander, HAASE,
Colonel-General

However, the divisional commander at his headquarters at Envermu, a few miles south-east of Dieppe, was not particularly worried. He did not think that an invasion would be attempted at this late hour, but he was determined to keep everyone on their toes until all danger of such an occurrence had passed. The High Command had been anxious about the situation during the summer and had been urging on the completion of the defensive works along the coast. In spite of many difficulties and delays due to shortages of labour and materials, the work had reached a point where he considered Dieppe to be almost impregnable to attack, either from the sea or from landward. A series of concrete bunkers and well-sited pillboxes covered all approaches to the town from inland, and a strong perimeter fence of barbed wire stretched from Puys on the east side to Pourville on the west, passing across the race-course and extending out almost to Petit Appeville in the southwest. The Dieppe beach was heavily wired and commanded by a variety of artillery, mortars and machine-guns, all protected by strong concrete defences. The other beaches in his divisional area were equally well protected by the same system of perimeter defence.

The general was not too happy about the siting of some of the heavy coastal defence batteries outside the Dieppe perimeter, but his objections had been overruled by the artillery people, who said the guns were placed in the best possible positions to cover the sea approaches.

During the afternoon of 18th August a signal arrived from Army H.Q. ordering the cancellation of the alert as from that night. The general discussed the order with his Chief of Staff, and decided that the cancellation was premature. 'They can still come in the morning,' he said, 'the alert stands until tomorrow.'

During the evening there was a noticeable atmosphere of relief at Divisional H.Q. The trying alert period was almost over. Tomorrow home leave would commence. Whatever the fears of the ordinary soldier, the staff were firmly of the belief that no attack would now take place. They went to bed or to their various duties with easy minds.

In the defence posts and look-outs covering the shore line there was no relaxation of tension, all positions were manned as usual and keen eyes peered seawards scanning the dark water for a sign of movement. A quarter moon was dropping towards the horizon, its intermittent, wan light seeming to accentuate the darkness below. The beach and sea verge, a faint glimmer in the dimness, were silent but for the sough and swash of the surf. As each sentry was relieved the invariable report was 'All quiet'.

Between its sentinel cliffs Dieppe slumbered, the tall houses blank with shuttered windows, the darkness and silence of the narrow streets unbroken.

Away across the Channel in England, 18th August had a very special significance for many men. Men of the 2nd Canadian Division, men of Nos. 3 and 4 Commando Groups, men of the Royal Marine Commandos, a few men of the

American Rangers and men of the Royal Navy, manning a variety of ships. All that day, these men were assembling in various South of England ports and embarking on the large troop-carriers and R. boats which would take them to sea. Farther inland, at many airfields, young pilots and air crews were being briefed for the major effort that lay ahead of them on the morrow.

By early evening every ship was loaded and ready for sea, and without fuss they slipped their moorings and set off. Once at sea the men were served a hot meal, and settled down as well as they could. They had been through this performance many times before, making practice landings on different beaches, and about six weeks before had been at sea and briefed as to their objectives when they were returned to port and disembarked. In spite of the briefing, some thought it all part of an elaborate scheme, while others knew it was the real thing, cancelled because the convoys had been detected then attacked by German aircraft.

Now they were off again, and any doubts about this particular mission were quickly dispelled when they were told where they were bound for. The men were incredulous – Dieppe again, and so soon after the last time? It seemed impossible that the top brass could be so stupid as to think the Germans hadn't got wind of the first attempt. Everyone had been given leave when they came ashore, and with some 5,000 men running loose around England, there must have been some inadvertent breaches of security. The enemy would be sitting waiting for them. The briefing said it was believed there were not many troops in the area. 'Get off the beach quickly and it will be a push-over.'

For many of these men, this day, now drawing to its close, had a very special significance. They could not know it, but for more than a thousand of them this was their last day. Tomorrow – in the morning – they would die.

Realization

In the early morning of 19th August, 1942, the inhabitants of Dieppe were awakened by the noise of gun-fire coming from seawards. Those whose houses commanded a sea view to the north-east and who took the trouble to get out of bed saw gun-flashes on the horizon about ten miles out from the coast. The time was just past a quarter to four, and by 4.15 the firing had ceased and all was quiet once more.

Although they did not know it, the people of Dieppe had just heard the opening bars in a symphony of death which was to rage about their ears for the next nine hours. Most of them returned to their beds to snatch a few more hours of sleep before they had to face another day of occupation, with its problems and perplexities, all unaware that fast approaching their coast was an armada of 237 ships carrying a force of more than 6,000 men, about to engage in one of the most desperate ventures of the war.

Dieppe settled back to sleep and even the German guards in their concrete emplacements relaxed somewhat. No general alarm had been given, so the cannonade was none of their concern. They noticed that the harbour lighthouse had begun to flash its subdued beam, obviously to guide in some shore-hugging vessels – a further sign that all was well. The time was 4.30 a.m.

Fifteen minutes later the sound of air-raid sirens and the far-off hum of aero-engines was heard coming from Pourville way, and almost at once the distant thudding of ack-ack guns caused doors and windows to rattle in their frames. Many people got up and started to dress – early as it was it seemed likely that they would have to go to the shelters at any moment. Looking from their windows they could see the western sky lit by flickering patterns of light from the guns, and as they watched, vicious stabs of flame tore the darkness to the east, in the direction of Puys, accompanied by a growing thunder of gunfire. Inured as they were to the sounds of war after two years in the front line, they were quick to detect a different note in the noise, a growling, crackling undertone that seemed fraught with menace. This was no ordinary air raid such as they were used to – this was something big and they were in the middle of it. Outside in the dark streets German soldiers could be heard running to their posts, calling exitedly to each other, and while the citizens waited wonderingly, the Dieppe sirens suddenly wailed out. It was nine minutes past five o'clock, and as the last notes of the sirens died away the low growl of distant aircraft was heard, rapidly swelling to a roar and then to an ear-splitting bellow as a multitude of planes came diving out of the north on to the town.

At once the dark sky was split and torn by flashes and criss-crossed by innumerable ribbons of tracer as the anti-aircraft guns roared out, adding their staccato bark to the crash of bombs exploding on the sea front. The noise was terrifying – a stunning cacophony of sound which struck terror into the hearts of all but the boldest.

Still dazed by their rude awakening, many people ran for the shelters, while others went to their cellars where they crouched white-faced and trembling at the violence of the storm raging over their heads.

For the space of five minutes aircraft bombed and machine-gunned the sea front and the hotels lining it, and as the last plane roared away over the roof-tops the dark horizon to seawards was lit with wicked flashes of gun-fire as invisible warships opened fire on the town. The booming of their guns and the crash of the shells exploding on the sea front continued for about five minutes, and then was almost drowned in a deafening uproar of gun-fire close at hand, the thunder of heavy artillery mingling with the mad chatter of machine-guns and the incessant thump of mortars.

What was happening nobody could tell, but some of the more courageous or foolhardy posted themselves at upper windows in an endeavour to see what was taking place. Those whose vantage points commanded a sea view could see little because the whole of the mile-long beach was obscured by thick fog or smoke, but overhead in the grey light of dawn, illuminated by flares and shell bursts, could be seen myriads of aircraft flying just above the chimney-pots. The sky seemed full of them, and the continuous roar of their motors formed a background of noise which was to last for hours. In the shelters there was much excited speculation. Could this be the invasion that they had all looked forward to but in their hearts dreaded? Old men, veterans of the 1914–18 war, were positive that the German guns commanding the beach were in action, and that could mean only one thing – the British were landing. From time to time fresh arrivals at the shelters were besieged for news of events outside, but most of them were too shaken and frightened to have any coherent stories. Some had seen German soldiers manning machine-guns at street corners and all were agreed that the streets were highly dangerous because of the constant rain of shell splinters that fell.

The shelters were now full of people in various stages of undress, among them many German soldiers, some without their helmets. Outside, the gun-fire seemed louder than before. Many people who had not gone to the shelters, unable to contain their curiosity ventured into the streets in search of news, and soon rumours began to spread like wildfire through the town. 'The British have landed at Pourville, they are in Berneval, they are on our beach.' How or where these stories originated nobody knew, but soon the whole town was agog with excitement. A few people, with an entire disregard for their personal safety, tried to work their way down towards the sea front, where there seemed to be heavy fighting, but the German soldiers at all street crossings sent them back. They said the British were on the beach and might be in the town at any moment. It seemed that the invasion had come at last, but no one knew for certain what was afoot. At seven o'clock the roar of battle continued as loud as ever, overhead the never-ending stream of aeroplanes flew with their ear-splitting din, while the people enclosed and pressed down by the appalling racket could only wait and hope.

Many who had remained in their homes set about preparing breakfast and attending to the usual domestic tasks of the day. At this time gas was still available, though somewhat weak in supply, and in some parts of the town electricity was still on.

One of those prepared to brave the dangers of the streets

in a quest for news was Monsieur G. Guibon, President of the Friends of Old Dieppe. To his acute observation and careful recording we are indebted for much of the details of events in Dieppe during and after the battle. Like everybody else in the town, he had been awakened by the naval engagement in the small hours of the morning, and later, disturbed by the gun-fire coming first from the west and then from the east, had dressed and gone downstairs. He arrived in his hallway just as the bombardment of the sea front began, and there met the German soldier who was billeted on his home. The soldier was sheltering under the stairs and told him it was impossible to go out because of the falling ack-ack splinters, so M. Guibon returned upstairs and from a top window sought to follow the course of events.

Nothing could be seen to seawards, but overhead there seemed to be hundreds of aircraft flying low and skimming the roof-tops in a terrifying manner. They were directing their attack on the waterfront, and soon clouds of smoke, black against the grey of the dawn, were billowing up from the burning houses on the Boulevard Verdun.

M. Guibon's house in the centre of the town did not command a sea view, but it was obvious, from the terrible din coming from the beach, that fighting was taking place there, and that could only mean one thing – the British were landing, it was the Invasion.

M. Guibon rushed downstairs to warn his neighbours, but with splinters still falling in a steady rain outside, had to wait for a lull before venturing out. Keeping close to the wall he made his way along the street, visiting several houses and everywhere finding people very calm and going about their household chores as if nothing was happening. One lady was actually making jam. Relief from the almost unbearable tension was found in performing the routine tasks of the day. M. Guibon's news was received without excitement or hysteria. Everybody was determined to remain in their homes, come what may, until they were ordered to leave. It was quite possible that the Germans would force the population to evacuate the town, but until that came to pass they would not move. At the moment this area, being well back from the sea front, seemed comparatively safe, although splinters were falling steadily and shells frequently screamed overhead. If the position worsened, the residents could always go to the shelters or take refuge in their cellars.

There were many rumours in the streets of British landings along the coast, and some German soldiers guarding an intersection told M. Guibon that the British had landed on the Dieppe beach. The soldiers were very excited and were firing their rifles at the aircraft which constantly came roaring over the chimney-pots. Some people who came along said they had left the area of the railway station. As many houses had been hit by shells fired from the ships, and that serious damage had been caused at Janval at the rear of the town by shells aimed at a German battery in the vicinity. It was reported that there were many civilian casualties in this area. A few people had got through from the Rue de Sygogne and streets near the sea front, where it seemed most of the houses were wrecked and on fire. Some of these people had met and spoken to small groups of British soldiers, who had given them cigarettes and in some cases money. The British were searching for snipers and shooting them off roof-tops whenever they were located. There had been much firing in the vicinity of the St Rémy church and the cinema, but the locals thought there were not enough British troops in the town to make much impression on the large number of German soldiers who were moving towards the sea front.

As the morning wore on, the pattern of events appeared unchanged – the heaviest fighting was still concentrated on the beach and the noise of gun-fire seemed to be growing louder and nearer. Aircraft continued to fly over the town in large numbers and the crump of bomb-bursts mingled with the incessant bark of anti-aircraft guns, while over and above these noises swelled the roar of battle from the waterfront, rolling in great waves of sound and fury over the town, booming, crashing, crackling, as the various instruments in the great orchestra of death took up their parts. People could not move far from their own doors, but in spite of the falling ack-ack splinters many made their way in and out of their neighbours' houses, picking up news and rumours of the battle raging so close at hand. By nine o'clock it was becoming all too clear to the knowledgeable that things were not going well for the invaders. The steadily growing volume of gun-fire, the sight of artillery pieces proceeding at speed towards the beach instead of away from it, brought no reassurance to the populace. There was no sign of any large-scale infiltration of British troops into the town. Indeed, there were more Geman soldiers than ever in all the streets leading to the beach, many with machine-guns, and in some places large field-guns were firing from the roads out to sea.

Somewhere about nine o'clock there was startling news – the B.B.C. were broadcasting to the people of Dieppe telling them that the action was not an invasion attempt but only a *coup de main*. This information was received with a general feeling of disappointment not unmixed with relief.

About this time the first German planes were spotted over Dieppe and many people witnessed air battles fought at a very low level, but generally the constant flights of R.A.F. machines over the town were unmolested and seemingly untouched by the very heavy ack-ack fire directed at them. They were keeping up unremitting attacks on the German batteries behind the town and on the cliffs on either side. A railway worker said that a report from Arques told how, in the early morning, there had been a raid on the German guns sited just north of the village and several bombs had fallen among the houses, killing many people while they were still asleep.

Shorty after nine o'clock observers saw the castle on the West Headland under heavy shell-fire from the sea. This historic building, which had survived many battles in its time, now sheltered German machine-guns and a battery of field-guns. From their lofty eyrie the German gunners could enfilade the whole length of the beach, and though it was under continual bombardment from both sea and the air, it was not until near the end of the battle that its fire power was seriously reduced. Many buildings on the sea front were now burning and huge clouds of smoke were gradually drifting over the town, so that it became impossible to distinguish the markings of the low-flying aircraft. The noise of battle was undimished and behind the town the German batteries could be heard pounding away without cessation, their heavy projectiles clearly audible as they screeched over the town. Some of them fell grievously short of their intended targets, smashing into houses in the Rue Claude Groulard and setting them alight. This matter of short-fired shells was one of the major hazards of the day, the fire from the sea

26

being particularly inaccurate and causing a great deal of damage to civilian property as well as loss of life.

By eleven o'clock people had become accustomed to the infernal racket, and in the safer quarters of the town many housewives were endeavouring to prepare lunch for their families. All gas, electricity and water were now off, but fires were lighted and food cooked just as if the noise reverberating over the town was a summer thunderstorm instead of a major battle. About this time a changing tempo was noticeable in the sound of the guns. The incessant hammering of machine-guns had died away, except for occasional bursts, but there was much more artillery fire, the heavy detonations merging into a rolling, vibrating thunder that beat upon the brain and kept doors and windows rattling. A thick screen of smoke hung over the town so that it was impossible to see any distance. Aircraft were still pouring in, as numerous as ever, their motors blaring invisibly in the fog, but the staccato bark of the ack-ack guns had considerably diminished, and shell splinters no longer descended upon the streets. New stories were circulating among the people – the Casino had been captured by the British, the gas-works and the tobacco factory had been destroyed, many prisoners had been seen wearing Canada flashes on their shoulders, all the houses near the sea front were burning.

As midday approached, the cannonade reached an unprecedented degree of violence. What is presaged no one could tell. Some people assumed that further landings were taking place, but when the sudden shrill scream of ships' sirens was heard, cutting through the uproar of the guns like a whiplash, it seemed more likely that a withdrawal was under way. For more than an hour the terrific bombardment continued, shaking the very foundations of the town, while the mad bellow of aircraft and the crash of exploding bombs added to the indescribable din.

Quite suddenly the cannonade ceased and the crackling of small-arms fire was heard from the western end of the Promenade. People began to appear in the streets, but another terrific burst of gun-fire sent most of them scurrying indoors once more. For about five minutes the guns fired, then fell silent once more. Now there was nothing but occasional rifle shots from the beach and the ever-present aeroplanes roaring overhead. Spasmodic bursts of anti-aircraft fire came

27

from inland and the faint sound of cannon-fire could be heard from the direction of Pourville. Dieppe itself was quiet with a strange, uncanny quietness. The battle here was over, at least for the time. People flocked into the streets, but the German soldiers at street crossings would not allow them to pass. They gathered about their doorways in little groups, talking excitedly, relating their experiences and asking about friends and relatives. Parties of Canadian prisoners were now being escorted through the town, and as they passed, the local people became silent and looked at them with pity. The sight of a number of wounded men staggering along, pale and blood-stained, moved many of the onlookers to tears. On the Avenue Pasteur, leading to the hospital, a large number of prisoners were lined up, among them many wounded men on stretchers or lying on the ground. Their numbers were constantly being added to until there must have been 1,500 men in the avenue. It was said that they were to be immediately evacuated by train to Rouen.

Some people who had brought injured relatives to the hospital said conditions there were ghastly. The corridors were filled with wounded soldiers lying on the floors, awaiting attention, and more were being brought in every minute. British, German and civilian wounded were mixed up in a frightful pattern of torn flesh and shattered limbs. Nuns and attendants moved amongst them, affixing temporary dressings and endeavouring to alleviate their sufferings. Here was the dreadful aftermath of the battle in all its horror. In the town, traffic was now permitted and people were moving about freely, seeking out friends and relatives and gazing in astonishment at the wreckage of the streets. Some of those who lived near the waterfront had observed the early stages of the battle, and related how the landing-craft had approached the beach to discharge their human cargoes. The moment they touched down, the men had poured out, only to be shot down as they left the ships. Some of the vessels had landed tanks, which appeared not to be able to make progress on the steep shingle and remained on the beach firing their guns into the town.

A few people had actually met some Canadians and had been given leaflets addressed to the people of Dieppe, telling them to stay indoors and not to do anything which might provoke punitive action on the part of the enemy. Dieppe was a shambles. At the lower end of the Rue Gambetta the ground was littered with roof-tiles and fallen wires, and many houses had suffered damage from shell-fire. There were German field-guns in the street pointing seawards, and farther on in the Rue de Sygogne rubble and debris of every sort lay about – many houses here were completely gutted and hardly one had escaped damage. Some were still burning in spite of the efforts of the fire-fighters. Lying directly below the castle on the West Hill, the Rue de Sygogne had suffered heavily from the naval bombardment, many ill-directed shells striking the houses and the Regina Hotel on the corner. The inhabitants of this area were beginning to appear in the streets. They looked haggard and dazed, and were visibly affected by their terrible experience. For nine hours they had been in the forefront of the battle, their streets swept by gun-fire and their houses struck by shells and bullets. As was inevitable, some had been killed and almost all had stories of narrow escapes as shells plunged through their roofs and bullets lashed the walls and windows. Many, of course, had spent the day in cellars or shelters and had little or no idea of what had taken place. Coming out to find their homes in ruins proved too much for some of the women, who were led away weeping bitterly while their husbands stood in stunned silence before all that was left of their once comfortable homes. The Rue Descalliers, behind the Boulevard Verdun, was a complete wreck, the road a maze of fire-hoses and most of the houses burnt out or still burning. The residents were moving out, some still dragging pieces of furniture from their homes and piling them in the road.

They related how a group of Canadians had burst into the street and rushed through the houses to attack the hotels on the Boulevard Verdun from the rear, while another group had run towards the docks. There had been some rifle-fire in the Place Mouliná Vent, where it seemed most of the party had been made prisoners.

The houses in the Rue Descalliers had been damaged in the first air-attack on the sea front and later had been repeatedly struck by shells from the ships. Owing to insufficient water pressure, the fire-fighters were unable to control these fires or the fire at the tobacco factory near by, which people said had been set alight by some very accurate

29

shelling from the sea. They were rather disgruntled about this, as they did not consider it a military target, and when someone said there were 140 tons of tobacco destroyed they were loud in their lamentations. In this area many houses in the streets leading to the sea front had been badly damaged, as had the houses on the Quai Henry IV, the latter by fire from the German guns in the Pollet cliffs to the east. All was now quiet in the town except for the noise of German aircraft, which were flying over in large numbers. A thick pall of smoke hung above the roof-tops, drifting slowly south-east before the freshening wind. It was announced that curfew would be at eight o'clock, and many people who had not had any food all day ran about seeking to buy provisions. Not many shops were open, and those that were had long queues of patient customers standing quietly in the street, not talking very much, still rather dazed by their nightmare experience.

Few people slept well in Dieppe that night – with ears still ringing with the racket of battle and nerves stretched to breaking-point, they lay awake listening to the rumble of heavy vehicles through the usually quiet streets. All night long the traffic continued, as tanks, lorries and mobile artillery poured into the town.

People awaited the dawn with apprehension – would there be another attack? During the early hours of the morning it began to rain heavily, and the dawn broke grey and misty, but without incident. By eight o'clock the rain had ceased and the streets quickly became alive with people. The buses, which had not run the day before, now appeared as usual and from the station the noise of trains could be heard. Life was quickly returning to normal, despite the large number of German troops and vehicles which cumbered the roads. Shopkeepers were cleaning up in front of their stores, most of which were open for business, and housewives were out with their shopping-baskets. The soldiers did not interfere with the movement of the towns-folk except in the streets parallel to the waterfront, where many houses were still burning in spite of the efforts of the fire-fighters, who were greatly hampered by lack of water. Had the supply been adequate many premises could have been saved the day before, as the firemen showed rare cour-age in tackling blazing buildings during the height of the battle. On several occasions they found themselves caught between the opposing forces, and one unit, while moving into position near the City Hall, had been fired on by a tank on the Promenade, fortunately without damage or casualties.

Everywhere there was life and movement, people talking excitedly and congratulating one another on having come through the battle unscathed. Many from the outlying districts and the country around Dieppe were now in town, viewing with awe the burnt-out buildings and littered streets. Listening to the dreadful uproar and seeing the huge clouds of smoke billowing over the town on the previous day, they had thought Dieppe was completely destroyed.

M. Guibon, who had spent the previous day dodging shell splinters as he went about reassuring and encouraging his neighbours, now set off on a tour of the town, interviewing people and gathering details of the battle as he went along. It was surprising how many people knew nothing. They had remained hidden in the shelters all day and had seen nothing of the action, but there were many who had stayed in their homes and had stories to tell. Gradually a picture began to emerge from the welter of information, often accurate, which was eagerly proffered by the citizens. Bullet-riddled buildings and smashed windows told their own tale of gun-battles in the streets and made it possible to trace the depth of penetration into the town by the invaders. It seemed that some small groups had progressed as far as the Rue de la Barre and the Grande Rue, and the area between these streets and the sea front had been the scene of much fighting. Residents who had spoken to the Canadians said they were in high fettle and eager to get to grips with the Germans. For a short while they succeeded in clearing the streets of the defenders, but were not in sufficient numbers to resist for long, and those that were not cut off and captured apparently withdrew to the beach. There was a story current of a group of armed men in civilian clothes having fired on the Canadians, but it was not possible to ascertain who these civilians were.

Access to the sea front was still *verboten*, but from the upper windows of the badly-damaged City Hall it was possible to view the whole of the main battlefield. It was a gruesome sight — torn and shattered shingle strewn with corpses

31

in the pitiful attitudes of death, some hanging from the broken wire, some huddled in little hollows where they had sought in vain for shelter from the relentless rain of steel that beat upon them. Here and there the stones had been scooped up against the sea wall, as if to protect the troops crouching beneath its cover.

Directly opposite the Casino a large tank-landing-craft with the No. 5 on its side lay high and dry with tanks close by, some with broken tracks, some with smashed turrets. One large tank on the beach near the Casino was reported to have fired continually on the gun position on the West Headland and to have played a major role in silencing the battery on the terrace of the castle.

Farther along was another tank-landing-craft and right at the end of the beach under the pier was a third. Smaller landing-craft lay about, some half submerged, and many derelict tanks were scattered about the beach. The shingle was littered with abandoned weapons and equipment, which were being collected into piles by German soldiers. More Germans were to be seen clambering over and the stranded vessels. On the lawns and the Maritime Boulevard were five large tanks, one of which appeared to have dropped into some kind of tank-trap. Many khaki-clad bodies lay about in the long grass, with Germans going through their pockets.

It was a scene of the utmost desolation and horror, yet it was difficult to tear oneself away from it. Here only a few short hours ago men had died in hundreds – burrowing in the shingle, crouching under the sea wall, pitting their shrinking flesh and puny weapons against a deluge of hot steel that ripped and tore the life from them. Their mute bodies bore witness to the sacrifice they had made, and as the full implication of their agony struck home the watchers in the windows stood silent and white-faced.

Later in the day French municipal workers arrived with lorries and commenced the work of removing the dead Canadians, who were interred in a common grave in the cemetery. The Germans had already removed their own dead, the bodies of the soldiers being cremated while officers and N.C.O.s were buried separately in a special plot.

As the Canadian dead arrived at the cemetery the Germans searched each body, removing boots, papers and any valuables found. When the grave was finally filled in, a

German firing party arrived to pay their last tribute to the dead, while an officer placed a wreath in position. Later hundreds of wreaths and sheaves were brought by the local people, so that the huge mound was entirely covered by flowers.

Everywhere throughout the town people were cleaning up in front of their homes. Many roofs had been stripped of slates by blast and the roads were littered with debris and broken glass. Hundreds of windows had been broken and householders were pasting sheets of paper over the apertures. Some of the worst damage was in the suburbs of de la Barre and Janval, where many houses had been destroyed or badly damaged by bombs and shells aimed at the German batteries in the vicinity. Twelve of the residents had been killed and many more injured. It was said that a large number of Germans had been killed here when a school in which they were stationed had been bombed. The German guns had been under constant attack from an early hour, and the fields and roads in the district were pitted with large craters. Civil Defence workers were still searching among the ruined houses for people who had been reported missing. All the roads leading into Dieppe were crowded with convoys of tanks and lorries. People living outside the town said that from an early hour on the 19th German traffic had been moving in towards Dieppe. A large number of artillery weapons had been noticed, also many omnibuses and trucks evidently commandeered by the Germans to transport their troops. The general opinion was that the British would not have progressed far inland against such a concentration of forces.

At Gueures a company of German cyclist troops had just arrived back from Pourville. These men had left Gueures early the previous morning, when the sounds of battle were becoming audible from the coast. They were now unshaven and dishevelled and appeared very dispirited. The local people concluded gleefully that they had been badly mauled by the invaders, and the men admitted freely that they had encountered very fierce resistance from the Canadians. They had been in action most of the day and standing to arms all night, and were obviously very tired, which probably accounted for their depressed condition. From them it was learnt that the British had penetrated inland for nearly three

33

miles, as far as Petit Appeville, and had then withdrawn to Pourville from whence they re-embarked, leaving a rear-guard who had continued to fight until late in the afternoon. They only surrendered when down to their last shot. These Germans seemed much impressed by the fighting quality of their opponents.

The condition of Pourville was indescribable. The streets were littered with the usual debris of broken glass and roof-tiles. Houses were burnt out or badly damaged, with walls chipped and pock-marked from bullets. The village had been under heavy mortar and machine-gun fire for many hours as the British fought to hold open their line of escape. The fighting had started in the early hours, when the van-guard of the invaders had encountered a German de-tachment in the main street and killed the majority of them, and from that time until late in the afternoon the battle had raged in and round the houses. With nowhere to go, the inhabitants had hidden in their cellars or back rooms, often with Canadians firing from the windows overhead. Inevi-tably some had been killed and injured, and the survivors were clearly suffering from the after-effects of their dreadful experience. The sea front and beach bore witness to the fierce-ness of the fighting. Blood-stained shingle was dotted with the bodies of the Canadians who had fallen at the first attack or later when endeavouring to board their ships. Eye-wit-nesses said that most of them had been killed when trying to escape as the Germans were firing on the beach from the high ground at each end. It was said that towards the end the British had cleared everyone out of their houses and made an attempt to set them on fire, but the incendiary bombs proved defective and the population were spared this final blow. Everyone remarked upon the courage and bearing of the Canadians, who drank coffee with the people, gave them cigarettes and apologized for disturbing them in such a dras-tic manner. The people living in the few scattered farms in the open country inland from Pourville had an anxious time. Some of them were fired on as they went to work in the fields, and near Ouville ground-strafing R.A.F. fighters wounded some workers as they ran for shelter. One farmer, driving his herd of cows to the milking-shed in the early morning, was caught by three planes who dropped bombs on and around the road in his vicinity. When he recovered his senses he found his cattle dead on the road and in the adjoining fields. Over towards Hautot, where the raiders had captured and destoyed a battery near Bernouville Wood, the local residents took some British wounded into their houses and bandaged up their hurts as well as they could.

On Friday, 21st August, the Dieppe Civil Defence people were ordered by the Germans to proceed to Puys and Berneval to remove the dead from the beaches. This was a particularly unpleasant task, as the bodies had been lying there for three days and the stench of corruption was in the air. Many of the dead men were equipped with bags containing grenades, and when the first body was lifted a grenade dropped on the stones and exploded, wounding three of the workers. The French thereupon refused to handle any more bodies until German specialists had taken away the grenades. After some argument the grenades were removed and the gruesome work proceeded. Some two hundred dead Canadians were taken from Puys beach and about forty Commandos from Berneval. The residents of Puys were very indignant because the wounded Canadians had been left unattended on the beach until late in the evening. The Germans made no effort to pick them up and would not allow the French to do so. The village was not damaged but had been strafed by British fighters after the surrender, and one woman was killed.

The inhabitants had been awakened from sleep in the early morning by gun-fire out to sea, and hearing the German troops running through the streets to their posts, had stayed awake, feeling that something was about to happen. About five o'clock some watchers had seen a flotilla of small craft approach, and as they neared the beach, the German guns opened a terrific fire on them, both from the sea wall and from either flank. As the men tried to get ashore they fell in dozens at the water's edge, and seemingly only a few managed to climb to the top of the high sea wall, where their bodies were found in the wire. The Germans said they had captured about a dozen in a wood to the west of the village. The guns at the beach were firing without ceasing for about three hours, and the first of the prisoners arrived in the village about nine o'clock. At Berneval much the same thing happened – the troops landed in daylight and the Germans were waiting for them. Some succeeded in getting

35

off the beach into a narrow lane but could go no farther. They fought on here for hours and were eventually made prisoners. A few reached Petit Berneval, and were hidden in houses by the locals, but were discovered by Germans who came searching with dogs.

These men were English Commandos and had with them an American officer, whose body was found in the lane. They came in six landing-craft, all of which were sunk when they returned to evacuate their troops. This attempt was presumably directed against the coastal battery near Berneval and was a complete failure, but people were talking about a small party of Commandos who had got ashore at Belleville from one vessel. They were seen in Berneval-le-Grand, where people directed them to the German battery, which they proceeded to attack and put out of action for nearly two hours. The only shells the Germans fired during this time were some aimed at their attackers. The little party made good their escape, followed by some young Frenchmen who begged to be taken to England.

M. Guibon, who kept a careful chornicle of events in Dieppe during and after the raid, mentions that by the week-end life had returned to normal and people were going about their business as though nothing had happened. The stories grew and multiplied and, as M. Guibon says, 'it was difficult to control the truth of the given facts'. Among the many fantastic stories circulating was one about people having met several Canadian soldiers running through the town in their underwear, minus uniforms and rifles. This story was not believed, but strangely enough it happened to be true.

Although the return to normalcy was general, there were many individuals whose lives were changed to a lesser or greater degree by the events on 19th August: people who had seen sudden and violent death in their familiar streets, a few who had witnessed the mass carnage on the beach, those whose homes had been destroyed and those who had seen their loved ones killed or maimed – happenings which are not to be easily forgotten and which would darken their thoughts and minds for many a long day. People were appalled at the futility of it all – death and wounds and destruction, and at the end nothing achieved. The question uppermost in the minds of the French people at this time was, Why?

The propaganda machines of both sides were now busy answering this question, and the French people were subjected to a barrage of radio and press reports and statements.

Apart from eye-witness accounts which were broadcast, many of them obviously untrue and inaccurate and clearly given by speakers who had not been within a hundred miles of Dieppe during the action, the German propaganda was very cleverly handled. Its main theme was that the attack was the spearhead of an invasion, which the British had been forced to undertake by pressure from Russia and against the wishes of America. The absence of American troops, except for a mere handful, lent weight to this latter assertion.

The German radio stated that on the afternoon of the battle, while the defeated troops were straggling back across the Channel, German reconnaissance planes had located a large convoy of vessels crammed with soldiers returning to Portsmouth. This was presumed to be part of the main invasion force intended to follow up a successful seizure of Dieppe. This news was followed by a statement that landings had been attempted on other parts of the Normandy coast and all had been thrown back with heavy losses.

Meanwhile the French people, seeking desperately for the truth, kept their radios tuned in to London to hear a series of laconic broadcasts stating that the action was merely a *coup de main*, a reconnaissance in force. The whole trend of British announcements was so vague and, to the people of Dieppe at least, so inaccurate, that they began to wonder if there was not some truth in the German viewpoint. As for the rest of France – deluged with German propaganda, puzzled and bewildered – they gradually came to believe, albeit with regret, that an invasion attempt had met with a bloody ending.

While the radios of the world were buzzing with theories and speculations, the inhabitants of Dieppe settled down to count the cost of the affair. It would take weeks to assess the material damage, which almost certainly would run into millions of francs. All the buildings on the sea front and many of the houses in adjoining streets were badly damaged or totally destroyed. The tobacco factory was ruined; all over the town houses had been wrecked by stray shells; hardly a pane of glass was left intact; innumerable roofs were damaged by shell fragments or stripped of tiles by blast; telephone and power lines were torn down and water mains broken. Of the civil population some fifty had been killed and over one hundred injured. Serious enough, in all conscience, but it could have been immeasurably worse, considering the colossal amount of shot and shell fired over and above the town for nine hours.

Both the British and the Germans congratulated the townspeople on their exemplary behaviour during the battle, and Hitler announced that a relief fund would be opened at once. Some 10,000,000 francs were collected and divided between Dieppe and Rouen, which had suffered heavily in an air-raid on the 18th. Hitler also released many French soldiers, prisoners of war, whose homes were in the area of Dieppe. On the other hand, many young Frenchmen from the neighbourhood were arrested on suspicion of having favoured the invaders. Indeed, some of them had besought the British to take them back to England, and somehow this became known to the Germans. One French youth had got as far as the beach at Pourville and had been killed. Regarding their battered town and reflecting on the events of that tragic day, the Dieppois were of the opinion that the whole enterprise was ill-judged and crazy. As one Frenchman put it, 'You don't have to be a brass hat to know that to land on a beach like Dieppe, where the natural features so favour the defences, is asking for trouble.'

Gestation

AFTER the ignominious ejection of the British Army from France in June 1940, Britain found herself forced on to the strategic defensive and in mortal danger of invasion. However, this unhappy position did not deter active minds (of which Winston Churchill's was the most active) from planning how best to resume an offensive spirit and find ways and means of harassing the enemy, now committed to the defence of an enormous coastline, extending from the far north of Norway to the Franco-Spanish frontier.

Throughout her long history of wars against the continent of Europe, as far back as Drake's time, Britain had employed the technique of raiding, and here lay the answer to the present problem – amphibious raids on the enemy shores, mere pin-pricks perhaps, but enough to compel the Germans to tie up large forces to guard their vulnerable coast. The psychological value of such attacks would be very great, although the amount of actual damage inflicted might be negligible. It was appreciated that a special force would be required to carry out these raids, and as the result of a brainwave of a staff officer, Lt.-Col. Dudley Clarke, the Commandos came into existence.

Theirs was the task of carrying the war into enemy territory, and they had the whole-hearted support of the Prime Minister, at no time a believer in passive resistance. To control and direct the new force, Combined Operations H.Q. was formed, under the command of Lt.-Gen. Bourne. The embryo group staged its first operation on 24th June, 1940, the day after France surrendered, in the shape of an attack on the Boulogne area, but nothing of any importance was achieved. Thereafter various small raids were carried out against enemy-held coastlines from Norway to France. Gen. Bourne was later succeeded by Admiral of the Fleet Sir

Roger Keyes, who remained in charge until he was retired in November 1941 to make way for Lord Louis Mountbatten, who became Chief of Combined Operations, with the rank of rear-admiral. Under the dynamic direction of the young Chief, C.O.H.Q stepped up the pace, their most important operation being the attack on St Nazaire in March 1942.

By this time Germany was deeply involved in her onslaught on Russia, and all danger of an invasion of Britain had passed. America was an active ally, girding herself for the momentous struggle ahead, while at home thought was already being given to the inevitable invasion of western France. The Planning Committee of Combined Operations H.Q. were busy with various projects, one of which is worthy of comment if only because of its fantastic nature. This was a scheme to land a complete division with a regiment of tanks somewhere in the Pas de Calais area. The tanks would strike inland to attack the German H.Q. West outside Paris, and having accomplished their mission, return to the coast and, together with the troops, re-embark for home. Needless to say, this plan did not find favour with higher authority. One other plan, however, was given serious consideration at top level. This was Operation 'Sledge-hammer', which proposed to establish a permant bridge-head in the Pas de Calais area during the summer of 1942.

The over-all political and strategic situation at this time was difficult. In May the Germans had renewed their offensive on the eastern front, and everywhere the Russians were being driven back. There was the ever-present fear that Russia would be forced out of the war altogether, something which would be a disaster of the first magnitude to the Allies. Stalin had never ceased to call for a second front in Europe, and now his demands became insistent. The Americans, who earlier had agreed with Britain to throw all their efforts into the war against Germany and to relegate the Japanese war to second place, were anxious to get on with the job and were pressing for an immediate large-scale landing in western France. Winston Churchill, while fully realizing the need to take some of the weight off Russia, could not agree with an invasion of Europe at that time, maintaining that in their present state of unreadiness the Allies would simply invite disaster and another Dunkirk. His plan called for an attack on North Africa, where the resistance likely to be encountered from the Vichy French would be negligible. As we know, the North African venture was eventually agreed to, but this did not prevent the Americans from continuing to advocate an emergency landing in France; indeed, President Roosevelt went so far as to suggest what he called 'a sacrifice landing'.

They had received the 'Sledgehammer' plan with enthusiasm, and were greatly chagrined when, in July 1942, Mr Churchill finally vetoed it, on the grounds that any such action would prove to be a bottomless pit into which Britain would pour her reserves of manpower and material. Indeed, so annoyed were the Americans that Mr Secretary Stimson, backed by some American generals, suggested to Roosevelt that he should revoke the policy of all-out war on Germany and switch instead to Japan. Fortunately the President proved himself wiser and more far-seeing than his hot-tempered advisers, and scouted the suggestion. It is only fair to say that later these same advisers had the grace to acknowledge that they were wrong and Mr Churchill right.

The American attitude probably arose from the fact that the President, in a moment of irresponsibility, had promised Molotov in person that a second front in Europe would be opened in 1942. This must have caused some embarrassment to the British Government, who countered by handing Molotov a note affirming their desire and intention to open a second front speedily, but *giving no promise as to when this would be done.*

They did, however, give an assurance that a large-scale attack against the French coast would be mounted in the early autumn and would be followed by other similar operations, which it was hoped would keep the enemy in doubt as to the British intentions and cause him to draw off troops and aircraft from the eastern front.

German disposition maps of the time show that they had 206 divisions on the eastern front, forty-six in France and seven in North Africa. One can hardly blame the Russians for thinking they were bearing more than their fair share of the war.

While these top-level arguments were raging between London and Washington, the Planning Committee of Combined Operations H.Q. were quietly discussing a scheme for a raid on the Dieppe area. Earlier that year the Army Chiefs of Staff had intimated that a large-scale attempt on the enemy coast, involving the use of tanks, was desirable in order to test the enemy reaction and to gain experience for application to the very much greater undertaking in the future. Indeed, they considered it not only desirable but absolutely necessary that such a rehearsal should be staged. The coming invasion of France would be on a vast scale. Nothing like it had ever been attempted before, and *it must not fail*. There were many lessons to be learnt, much new equipment and new techniques to be tried out, and while something had been gained from the many amphibious exercises carried out in Scotland and the West of England, it was thought that there were weaknesses and shortcomings which would only show up under actual battle conditions. It was also important to know what were the chances of getting a large fleet of assorted vessels across the Channel without detection by enemy air or surface craft, and maintaining them in sight of a hostile coast during many hours of daylight. The big danger was from aerial attack, and the R.A.F. welcomed the opportunity of bringing the Luftwaffe to battle on a large scale and of proving that they could afford adequate protection to both naval and ground forces.

In order to explore the German reaction to the full, the operation must present the outward appearance of an invasion attempt, which would imply using at least a division, together with a regiment of tanks.

At this period all plans for invasion were based on surprise landings on open beaches, with the rapid seizure of an adjacent port before the enemy had time to demolish or seriously damage the facilities. Dieppe seemed a natural target for such a try-out. First, it was not really large enough to serve as an invasion port and consequently had been ruled out by the planners for future use. Secondly, it was within reasonable range of the R.A.F. fighter bases in the South of England. And thirdly, it could be reached by an invading force under cover of darkness, an important point if tactical surprise was to be achieved.

With the idea approved in principle, the Planning Committee, together with some members of Home Forces G.H.Q. got down to work on the details. Two alternative plans were produced. One called for strong assaults on both flanks, with the centre kept under threat, and the other for flank attacks plus a strong attack by infantry and tanks against Dieppe itself. The first plan was discarded because the tanks would have to land at Quiberville, the only suitable beach apart from Dieppe, and to reach the centre would have to cross two rivers. The bridges might not be strong enough to bear the thirty-ton vehicles, or might be blown up, in either event leaving the tanks stranded miles away. Also, an encircling movement would be too slow and give the enemy time to prepare. It was therefore agreed to adopt the alternative plan, whereby parachute troops would attack the extreme flanks to destroy coastal batteries there, and landing would be made at Pourville and Puys to support a strong frontal attack on Dieppe. The assault would be preceded by a heavy air bombardment on the town. This plan was approved by the Chiefs of Staff early in May. Before this it had already been decided to use Canadian troops as the main force, and at the beginning of May the Officer Commanding Canadian Forces in Britain, General McNaughton, was told of the proposal. In due course he and his staff approved the plan, and Canadian officers had a hand in filling in the many necessary details.

The Canadian 2nd Division, under Major-General Roberts, was selected for the task. This division comprised the 4th Infantry Brigade, commanded by Brigadier Sherwood Lett, consisting of the Royal Regiment of Canada, the Royal Hamilton Light Infantry and the Essex Scottish Regiment; the 6th Infantry Brigade, under Brigadier W. W. Southam, consisting of Les Fusiliers Mont Royal, the Queen's Own Cameron Highlanders of Canada and the South Saskatchewan Regiment; the 14th Canadian Army Tank Regiment (the Calgary Regiment); a unit of the 1st Army Tank Brigade; light anti-air-craft and field-artillery detachments (the Toronto Scottish M.G., the Black Watch of Canada and Royal Canadian Artillery); over 300 Royal Canadian Engineers, and many administrative units.

The majority of these troops had been in England since 1940, deployed about the Southern Counties as an anti-invasion force. With the likelihood of invasion receding, the Canadians found themselves somewhat frustrated and considerably bored. They were often living under rather uncomfortable conditions, and the enforced inactivity brought about a lessening in discipline. There was an increase in crime – nothing very serious but young men in barracks didn't grow into plaster saints in 1942 any more than they did in Kipling's time. The situation overseas caused some slight concern to the Canadian Government, who were anxious that their Army should be given battle experience at the earliest possible moment. Now, at last, it seemed they were to get it.

The 2nd Division moved to the Isle of Wight early in May and at once went into special training – assault courses, practice embarkations and landings in all weathers, high-speed marches, and so on, all designed to harden the men for the tough work that lay ahead.

The original intention had been to stage the raid on 21st June, but a large-scale combined exercise held on the night of 11th–12th June went off badly. Units were landed on the wrong beaches, and some landing-craft were over an hour late in touching down. It was obvious that more training was urgently required. Another rehearsal was carried out on 22nd–23rd June, which went better, but there were still defects, particularly on the naval side, where difficulty was experienced in locating the correct beaches. Arrangements were now made to provide three special radar vessels equipped with special direction-finding apparatus, to lead some of the flotillas in to the French beaches. Once they were satisfied that the navigational weaknesses had been eliminated, final approval was given by the Canadian generals and it was decided to mount the operation at the first suitable opportunity early in July.

One important change in the original plan had been made. The heavy preliminary bombardment had been dropped. This would appear to have been a unanimous decision of the Planning Committee, the main reasons being that the R.A.F. could not be certain of hitting the small targets presented by the buildings on the sea front and the resultant damage to the town might prevent the tanks getting through, also such an attack would serve to alert the enemy. Another reason was that night bombing of French towns was prohibited by the Government, although this rule had been relaxed for this particular operation. It was appreciated that the French would be very much upset if Dieppe was smashed up and many people killed for what was after all only a small affair. How much this latter consideration weighed with the planners we do not know, but instead of a heavy air-attack it was agreed that the destroyers and cannon-fighters of the R.A.F. should attack the beach defences just before the troops touched down.

The R.A.F., commanded by Air Vice-Marshall Leigh-Mallory, would provide massive air cover and give ground support to the troops, while the Royal Navy guaranteed to get the force to its various destinations on time and bring it away again. The naval flotilla, comprising eight destroyers and numerous motor boats and gunboats, would be under the command of Captain Hughes-Hallet, who had been in on the planning of the enterprise from an early stage. This officer had spent a month, as Private Hallett, training with the Cameron Highlanders of Canada in order to find out what such an operation looked like to the Army. According to the Camerons' Regimental History, he is remembered as a good soldier and a bad card-player.

One of the destroyers, H.M.S. *Calpe*, was equipped to act as H.Q. ship, and from her Captain Hallet and General Roberts would control the action.

The attack would be launched on a front of eleven miles, extending from Berneval in the east to Quiberville in the west. There would be five main assaults, dividing into eight separate points, code-named as follows:

LEFT FLANK	Berneval	Yellow 1
	Belleville	Yellow 2
INNER LEFT	Puys	Blue
CENTRE LEFT	Dieppe	Red
CENTRE RIGHT	Dieppe	White
INNER RIGHT	Pourville	Green
RIGHT FLANK	Varengeville	Orange 1
	Quiberville	Orange 2

During the early summer these beaches and the country behind them were subjected to the most intense aerial reconnaissances, and maps and plans were prepared showing every detectable German gun position, tank-trap, pillbox and minefield.

The coast in the chosen area of attack comprises high, unscalable cliffs, broken in a few places by narrow valleys or gaps where rivers enter the sea. The largest of these openings is at Dieppe, where the River Arques runs out at the eastern end of a mile-wide cleft. It was only to be expected that these natural entrances from the sea would be well protected, and Dieppe itself particularly so.

Intelligence reports indicated that the town of Dieppe was garrisoned by two companies of infantry, and it was thought that it would take the enemy many hours to reinforce the area in any appreciable manner. The artillery at his disposal seemed very strong – three coastal-defence batteries: one at Berneval with three 17-centimetre guns and four 105-millimetre guns; one at Varengeville with six 15-centimetre guns, and one before Arques-la-Bataille with four 15-centimetre guns. In addition there were four four-gun batteries, two behind Dieppe and one on either side of the town. The Berneval battery was code-named Goebbels and the Varengeville battery Hess.

Also, the headlands flanking Dieppe beach were heavily fortified. The West Headland, code-named Hindenburg, had been fairly accurately assessed, but that on the east, called Bismarck, was something of a mystery. There was evidence that the Germans had installed machine-guns in caves dug into the side of the cliffs, but nothing definite was known. The hotels facing the sea had been fortified, and the Casino at the western end of the sea front was a strong point. In addition, all along the coast were concrete pillboxes hiding machine-guns and mortars covering the beaches. Buildings on the cliff tops at Puys, Berneval and Pourville were known to contain machine-guns, and it was a certainty that every foot of the coast where landings might be expected was covered by predicted fire from a variety of weapons.

Altogether a very tough nut to crack, but one which was thought by the planners to be not too tough.

By the end of June all was ready, and a suitable date early in July was selected for the raid. The troops were assembled and embarked, only for the weather to change, and they were kept cooped up in their ships for several days. 8th July was the last possible date in the month with a suitable combination of time and tide, and on the 7th the weather still remained unsettled and seemed likely to be so for several days. Then a new factor arose. Enemy planes spotted the assemblage of ships in the Solent and attacked it with bombs and machine-guns, fortunately causing only four minor casualties but damaging two of the troop-carriers. It is said that the attack would not have caused the abandoning of the operation, but the weather deteriorated even more and the expedition was finally cancelled. The disgusted and disappointed troops were disembarked and dispersed, many of them being given leave, and as all had been thoroughly briefed as to the nature of the affair a security problem immediately arose.

General Montgomery, G.O.C. South Eastern Command, advised that the operation be written off for good, but Combined Operations were not of the same mind. They had already had one other similar operation cancelled by higher authority and were deeply upset at the fate of the Dieppe plan, Operation 'Rutter', to give it its code name. They worked hard to have it revived and by mid-July it was once more approved, this time known as Operation 'Jubilee'.

When one considers the political and strategic situation at the time, it is not difficult to understand why the Dieppe raid was reinstated, even though in so doing the authorities were breaking their own rule of never returning to a target once a previous attempt on it had been cancelled. It is also possible that 'Jubilee' was considered a very effective screen for the coming invasion of North Africa, scheduled for November – which in fact it proved to be. In any event, 'Jubilee' was on, in spite of some people's misgivings and despite the very real risk that the Germans had got wind of the plan.

Some further changes were now made in the plan. For one thing, the points of embarkation were dispersed, to avoid any heavy concentration of shipping at one port; and for another, it was decided not to use parachute troops for the outer flank attacks, owing to their vulnerability to the weather. Instead, Commandos would be given the task of knocking out the two heavy coastal batteries. Goebbels and Hess, which together were quite capable of blowing the fleet lying off shore right out of the water. The detailed Plan of Battle was now as follows:

At 4.45 a.m. Commando Group No. 3, under Lt.-Col. Durnford-Slater, would land at Berneval and go for the Goebbels battery, while at the same time Group No. 4, under Lt.-Col. Lord Lovat, would go ashore at Quiberville and attack the Hess battery. Once these missions were completed, the two groups would re-embark and return to

England. Simultaneously with the outer flank landings, those on the inner flanks would go in: that on Blue Beach at Puys by the Royal Regiment of Canada, who would attack the field-battery behind the village and move on to the rear of the East Headland, and that on Green Beach at Pourville by the South Saskatchewan Regiment, who would secure the village, attack the rear of the West Headland and capture a fortified position known as Quatre Vents Farm, about one mile inland. Half an hour later the Cameron Highlanders of Canada would land at Green Beach and push forward inland to assault the airfield at St. Aubyn and the German H.Q. at Arques-la-Bataille. The Camerons would be supported by tanks coming from Dieppe. Finally, at 5.20 a.m., half an hour after the flank landings, the main assault would be made on the centre beaches, under cover of a brief bombardment from sea and air. The troops concerned were the Essex Scottish Regiment, who would attack Red Beach, left centre, and the Royal Hamilton Light Infantry, destined for White Beach, right centre. They would be supported by nine tanks landing at the same time, and the remaining tanks would come ashore at intervals until all were committed. In reserve would be the Fusiliers Mont Royal and the Royal Marine 'A' Commando. Once the beach was under control, the Marine Commando was to enter the harbour and seize or destroy invasion barges therein and any other likely targets. The two Canadian battalions would fan out to attack the headlands in support of the rear attacks, and move through the town with the tanks to the airfield.

With no stunning preliminary bombardment, the plan depended for success absolutely on the element of surprise. The various assault groups must be ashore and off the beaches within five minutes of zero hour. Any group more than fifteen minutes late could wreck the whole plan. The Royal Navy had the difficult and complex task of bringing a large armada of ships of many different types and varying speeds across seventy miles of water, through channels swept in enemy minefields, in total darkness and radio silence, to within a short distance of the French coast. There, many of the troops would have to trans-ship into landing-craft, form up into their respective groups and set out on the run-in, all within the very strictest time limit.

No less than 237 ships were required to transport and

escort the force, and sixty-seven squadrons of the R.A.F. were laid on to give fighter cover, provide smoke and support the ground troops with bombing attacks on enemy positions.

Artillery support and counter-battery action would also be provided by the destroyers with their four-inch guns, while close support in the early stages would be given by the numerous motor boats and support landing-craft armed with pom-poms and heavy machine-guns.

The troops were excellently equipped and armed, each man with his Mae West and 200 rounds of ·303 ammunition. Every last detail had been worked out, even down to the provision of bicycles for the platoon of Camerons who would go forward from the airfield to attack the German H.Q. at Arques. As one wag remarked, 'Just in case the local bus service is not running.' The striking force now comprised some 6,000 men, of whom about 5,000 were Canadians and the rest British Commandos, included in whose ranks were fifty American Rangers and some French Special Service men. Altogether a formidable force, capable of punching a sizeable hole in Hitler's West Wall – or so it was thought.

Frustration

AFTER the postponement at the beginning of July, weather conditions ruled out any further attempt until late in August. Time and tide would be right on the 18th and 19th. Now all depended on the weather. On the 17th a favourable forecast was received from the Met. people, covering the two following days. The order was given and Operation 'Jubilee' was on.

Last-minute photographic reconnaissances were flown over the beaches, final preparations were made and on the afternoon of the 18th embarkation began.

The troops and tanks sailed from five different south of England ports, Gosport, Southampton, Portsmouth, Newhaven and Shoreham, embarking as follows: No. 3 Commando Group in twenty-three assault craft (L.C.P.s); No. 4 Commando Group in the infantry landing-ship H.M.S. *Prince Albert*; the Royal Regiment of Canada in the landing-ships H.M.S. *Queen Emma* and *Princess Astrid;* the Black Watch of Canada and artillery units in the landing-ship H.M.S. *Duke of Wellington*; the Royal Hamilton Light Infantry and the Essex Scottish Regiments in the landing-ships H.M.S. *Glengyle, Prince Leopold* and *Prince Charles*; the South Saskatchewan Regiment in the landing-ships H.M.S. *Princess Beatrice* and *Invicta*; the Cameron Highlanders of Canada in twenty-five personnel landing-craft, Les Fusiliers Mont Royal in twenty-six personnel landing-craft, and the Royal Marine 'A' Commando in seven French Chasseurs and the gunboat H.M.S. *Locust*. The sixty tanks were carried in twenty-four tank landing craft, which also brought many of the Royal Canadian Engineers detachment and various small parties of other units. This fleet of assorted vessels was escorted by eight destroyers: H.M.S. *Calpe* (especially equipped to act as Headquarters ship and carrying the Naval Force Commander, Captain Hughes-Hallett, and the Army Commander, Major-General Roberts, in addition to the Air Liaison Officer, Air Commodore Cole, and some American officers, who were present as observers, H.M.S. *Fernie*, the reserve H.Q. ship with Brigadier Mann as senior Army officer, H.M.S. *Brocklesby, Gath, Albrighton, Berkeley, Bleasdale* and *Slazak*, the gun-boat *Locust* and the sloop *Alresford*, together with flotillas of motor gunboats, motor launches and flak ships.

This fleet was divided into thirteen groups, which sailed at varying times, and by nine o'clock all had cleared their home ports and were steadily converging to take up their stations behind a screen of sixteen minesweepers, which would guide them through a swept channel in a German minefield about half-way across. The moon was high, the sea calm, and all now depended on the sure navigation and seamanship of the Royal Navy personnel, whose job it was to get the fleet through safely and on time.

No easy task, with all those ships travelling at high speed in close company through the tricky half-light.

There were one or two narrow escapes from collision, but luck and skill succeeded, and by moonset they were out of the minefield. An hour later, at 3 a.m., the large troop-carriers commenced trans-shipping their human cargoes into the assault craft.

They were now within easy reach of the enemy coast, but so far the luck had held and no enemy air or surface craft had been detected. As the loaded assault craft manoeuvred in the pitch darkness and silence, some confusion arose as groups sought to make contact with their escorts and guide-ships. The minutes of darkness were slipping by – valuable minutes which if lost now could never be regained. Gradually the medley of little ships sorted themselves out and found their stations, but the group destined to land on Blue Beach lost their leading gunboat, and thirty valuable minutes passed before it was found.

By 3.30 a.m. four of the five groups into which the flotilla had divided were on their way towards the enemy coast ahead. They were well on time and only the sheerest bad luck could now divert them from their purpose. The fifth group was nearly twenty minutes late, minutes which could hardly now be picked up in the few short miles between them and their appointment on Blue Beach. Like the fingers of some colossal hand they radiated out towards France, long lines of ships filled with wondering men, taut, anxious, peering into the darkness for their first sight of the dark line which would be their destination.

On the extreme eastern flank of the fleet, twenty-three assault boats carrying No. 3 Commando Group followed steadily behind their guide ship, Gunboat No. 5, which was leading them to the Yellow Beaches at Berneval and Belleville. On either side of the convoy, invisible in the thick darkness, were a motor boat and a flak ship, and farther off to the east two destroyers patrolled on the look-out for enemy surface craft. The flotilla was on time and on course. One more hour and they would be in. From the gunboat keen eyes peered ahead into the blackness – they were very near the enemy coast now and anything could happen. And suddenly it did. Out of the blackness the silhouette of a darkened ship appeared almost dead ahead. A star-shell shot up, and there in the ghostly illumination were eight enemy vessels, steaming in line ahead towards Dieppe. Instantly the silence of the night was shattered by the crash of gun-fire as the enemy ships, altering course, concentrated their fire upon the gunboat. Struggling to reply, she was hit repeatedly, her forward guns silenced, her wireless-room wrecked, her engine-room damaged, so that she gradually lost speed and became a sitting target. Just in time, the flak ship, coming up at high speed, engaged the enemy and crippled two of them with her first salvoes. For perhaps twenty minutes a running fight ensued, with the German ships making off at speed for the safety of the coast, and then all was silent once more. The moment the first salvo thundered out, it seemed to the officers on the gunboat's bridge that all chance of secrecy was now lost. Whatever the result of the engagement, the cannonade would surely awaken the whole coast. By the worst of bad luck a chance encounter on the very threshold of success had put the whole mission in grave danger. But that was only the beginning of it – not only was the gunboat out of action, but the convoy of landing-craft had vanished, all but five of which had sought the protection of the gunboat at the first blast of gun-fire.

The Naval C.O., Commander Wyburd, and Lt-Col. Durnford-Slater, commanding the No. 3 Group of Commandos, took stock of the situation. It was clear that, with the convoy scattered, there would be no landing on the Yellow Beaches. Both men realized the importance of destroying the enemy battery at Berneval, but there was no hope of that now. The disaster must be reported to the H.Q. ship at once, but there was no means of communication. The gunboat, besides, was in grave danger, drifting helplessly almost in sight of the enemy coast. The decision was taken to set out in one of the landing-craft to find H.M.S. *Calpe,* while the other four vessels took the gunboat in tow back to England. With heavy hearts the two commanders embarked and for two hours cruised about searching for H.M.S. *Calpe.* Several ships were approached but none had wireless, and it was seven o'clock before they found their elusive quarry and reported the misfortune that had befallen their group.

The action had been observed from H.M.S. *Calpe,* where it was concluded that the two outlying destroyers had run into enemy vessels, while the two destroyers assumed the firing came from the shore. Nobody, apparently, ever thought that the convoy was in trouble. There was nothing *Calpe* could do, but it was a serious error of judgment on the part of the destroyers to treat the matter so lightly.

Meanwhile, the motor gunboat which had gone off in pursuit of the missing landing-craft had succeeded in rounding up five of them, and the little fleet was proceeding at full speed towards Yellow1, while a mile or two ahead of them, in the fast-fading darkness, a lone landing-craft made its way towards Yellow 2 at Belleville. Except for one other craft, all the others, finding themselves miles from the coast in daylight, returned home, many having been damaged and sustaining casualties before they got out of range of the naval battle. The solitary landing-craft heading towards Yellow 2 was one of five carrying No. 3 Troop of Commando Group 3. On board were the second-in-command of the group, Major Peter Young, Lt. Ruxton and two runners from Commando H.Q., Captain Selwyn and fourteen men of 3 Troop – nineteen men in all. When the naval action flared up on their port bow, Lt. Buckee, R.N.V.R., commanding the vessel, had kept his station at the head of the column of landing-craft following in the wake of Steam Gunboat No. 5. Buckee was aware that Commander Wyburd in the S.G.B. had determined to fight his way through any opposition encountered, but after an agonizing ten minutes it became obvious that this was not possible. Buckee's vessel was being raked by machine-gun fire from the enemy ships – to proceed was to court certain death. So, after a hurried consultation with Major Young, course was altered to starboard and they were soon out of range. Luckily no casualites had been suffered, although the canopy of the craft was riddled, but they were now alone – completely out of touch with the rest of the flotilla. Neither man had any doubt about their course of action. They had an appointment at Belleville and they intended to keep it. Their orders were to attack the Goebbels battery, and attack it they would. What matter if their numbers were few? Major Young had long taught the idea that a handful of men who meant business were worth any number of ordinary troops – and these men meant business. Their armament consisted of rifles, tommy-guns, one Bren gun, a two-inch mortar with six bombs and a three-inch mortar with four bombs. With these they would do all in their power to silence the powerful battery.

At fifteen minutes to five o'clock the vessel ran on to the beach and having asked Buckee to stand off the shore for as long as possible, the party set out on their desperate venture.

The only exit from the small beach was a steep and narrow cleft between the cliffs, which it had been intended to surmount with the aid of scaling-ladders. The cleft was choked with a mass of wire, and the men had no ladders, no Bangalore torpedoes, not even a wire-cutter. The way up seemed impossible to anyone but a Commando. Major Young said, 'We'll climb up on those stakes,' indicating the stakes driven into the side of the cleft to hold the wire. Leading the way, he started to climb, only to fall back on the man behind him. For a moment it looked hopeless, and somebody said so. That was enough for Major Young. As he admits himself, his stubborn nature took control, and using the barbed wire as a rope and the stakes as steps, he climbed steadily upwards, followed by his men. It was an unpleasant business, as the wire was very thick and the barbs were very close together, and soon the men's hands were a bloody mess. However, with the aid of some toggle ropes tied together the party reached the top safely.

So far there was no sign of the enemy and no sound of battle from either flank, but as they moved along the cliff they were cheered by the sight of five landing-craft and a motor boat approaching the beach at Berneval to their left. With the exception of one other craft, these five were all that remained of No. 3 Commando, now coming in to land at Yellow 1, in the full light of dawn.

Major Young got his party moving quickly into the cover of a small wood near the road leading into Berneval-le-Grand. He hoped to rendezvous at the village church with some of the Yellow 1 contingent, and going forward he studied the approach to the village through his binoculars. There were no Germans in sight, so he called up the party and they advanced down the road to the houses. On the way they met a young French boy on a bicycle, who gave them the best route to the battery and informed them that the Germans had 200 men there. The walk down the road in the quiet of the early morning was a strange experience. Dew was on the grass, birds were singing, and it was difficult to realize that they were deep in enemy territory. The quietness was suddenly shattered by a near-by blast of flak guns and the crash of bombs as a flight of aircraft came roaring over the battery, machine-gunning and bombing German gunners. The village street was full of frightened French people, who disappeared quickly when the file of grim-faced men came past. There was no sign of their comrades at the R.V., and while Major Young was endeavouring to get some men up in the church tower to snipe the battery, fire was opened on the party from a machine-gun. The fire was returned and the two-inch mortar fired off the six bombs with good effect, as the fire ceased. Finding there was no way up into the church tower, Major Young moved the party to the south or rear of the battery, but again coming under heavy fire from hidden positions, withdrew to the village. To the west of the battery was a large cornfield and this seemed to offer the best possibility for attack. The men were deployed in two lines in the corn, those in the rear line firing between those in front. The battery had been firing slowly – perhaps twenty shots at long intervals, rather as though the gunners were uncertain of their targets. From their position the Commandos were able to fire along the gun line, so that *all* the German gunners could hear *all* the bullets whistling past their heads – something which seemed to impress them considerably, because the battery did not fire again. After perhaps thirty minutes of this there was a roar, and a great cloud of black and yellow smoke billowed out about 200 yards ahead, as the Germans in their fury turned one of the heavy naval guns around to fire at the will-o'-the-wisp targets. Time after time the great cloud of smoke gushed out and shells screeched just above the Commandos' heads. But the gun could not be depressed enough to do any harm, and soon the firing ceased. For an hour and a half the Commandos kept up their attack on the guns, all the time being shot at by German riflemen in well-concealed positions, but either the enemy were poor marksmen or, as Major Young avers, a field of growing corn will stop a bullet, because nobody was hit.

However, this game could not continue indefinitely. At any moment tanks might appear from the south, against which the men had no protection. It seemed wiser to withdraw while the going was good. Captain Selwyn and a small party proceeded to the beach to establish a bridge-head and signal with Very lights if the landing-craft was still in the offing, while Major Young and Lt. Ruxton, with the Bren, moved off to shoot up an observation post on the cliff edge in front of the battery, which was likely to impede the embarkation. While they were exchanging long-range fire with the observation post, the Very light signals were seen and the two officers collected their men from the cornfield and retired to the beach. On the way back they were under fire both from the enemy and from M.L. 346, who obviously thought they were Germans, but they reached the beach unscathed, although here one man was injured through treading on a mine. They were now being heavily engaged by the observation post and troops on the cliff top, but, covered by the M.L., embarked without loss and were soon out of range. The withdrawal had been carried out only just in time. Although there were no tanks in the area, three companies of German troops, under Major von Blücher, had moved up to Berneval and were hard on the heels of Major Young's party. Lt. Buckee brought the landing-craft safely back to England in spite of a determined attack by a Ju.88.

This little gem of a Commando action, described by the

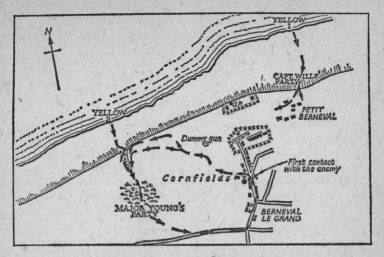

ATTACK ON GOEBBELS BATTERY BY NO. 3 COMMANDO

naval force commander in his report as 'perhaps the most outstanding incident of the whole operation', rendered ineffective the heavy German battery for more than two hours during the most critical phase of the landings on the main beaches, and earned for Major Young and Lt. Buckee the award of the D.S.O.

While Major Young and his little band were scaling the cliffs at Belleville, five landing-craft carrying part of No. 3 Commando Group were approaching Berneval. When the convoy scattered they had managed to keep together, and when found by their escorting motor boat were heading determinedly for their destination. The little force comprised two boat-loads of No. 6 Troop, one of No. 5, one of No. 2 and one with the H.Q. party, in all about a hundred under the command of Captain Wills, who had found himself the senior officer of all that remained of his group. Included were some American Rangers, led by nineteen-year-old Lt. Ed. Loustalot.

Representing less than a quarter of the force destined to attack the Goebbels battery, and fearing that all element of surprise had gone, they came out of the night into the greyness of the dawn to carry out their orders.

Where the rest of the group was they did not know, but as they neared the land it became obvious that they were the first to arrive. Berneval beach was quiet, strangely quiet. No Germans, no shots, just an expanse of grey stones backed by towering cliffs glimmering faintly in the early sun. Precisely at 5.15 a.m. the five craft touched down and the men leapt ashore, bracing themselves for the anticipated ordeal by fire. They had been warned to expect a pillbox on the beach and had brought a flame-thrower to deal with it, but nothing of the sort was seen, not a single shot broke the morning stillness, and there was no sign of the enemy until suddenly two German heads popped up over the cliff edge and as quickly disappeared. Now they had anything from five to ten minutes to get off the beach before the Germans appeared. Speed of movement was vital. Captain Wills, whose boat had landed a little ahead of the others, rushed his troop along the beach to the gully up which they planned to climb, only to find it completely blocked by a mass of heavy wire nearly fifty yards in depth and thickly studded with mines connected to trip wires. The wire was too deep to blow with their two Bangalore torpedoes, so a man got to work on it with wire-cutters. To the men inching their way through the wire the delay was agonizing. At any moment the enemy might appear on the cliff above and fire straight down at them, but at last it was done, and just as the final few strands parted a machine-gun opened fire on the beach, to be followed by others until it seemed that all hell had broken loose over their heads. Most of the fire seemed to be directed at the landing-craft, which were leisurely pulling off the beach, but bullets were twanging and whistling through the lower part of the wire, effectively preventing the bulk of the force from filing through the narrow gap in the wire. There was nothing for it but to attack along the cliff top and seek to draw the enemy fire from the beach. Accordingly Captain Wills led his troop out of the gully and against the German positions. The plan succeeded and shortly the rest of the Commandos were safely on the cliff top and moving inland. But now it was apparent that the Germans were wide awake and present in large numbers. Very heavy machine-gun and mortar fire was sweeping the ground, forcing the troops to take whatever cover they could find. For the moment the advance was held up.

Meanwhile, out at sea the motor boat M.L. 346 had observed a German ship approaching. This was the armed tanker *Franz*, a straggler from the convoy which had caused all the trouble earlier on, and she was now coming in with the obvious intention of driving the M.L. ashore. The German skipper handled his ship well, but the M.L., like a boxer slipping a punch, swerved away, and closing to thirty yards, engaged the enemy with such ferocity that in a few minutes she was ablaze and her guns out of action. Whether the fierceness of the attack upset the Germans or whether her steering-gear was damaged is not known, but the *Franz* continued at full speed for the shore, where she ran firmly aground on the rocks. Another landing-craft was now observed making for the shore under heavy fire from two large houses on the cliff. Swinging away, the M.L. turned the full force of her small guns on the enemy positions, and soon both houses were on fire and their guns silenced. The landing-craft ran in and landed her complement safely, but backing off into deep water, immediately sank. The new arrivals, a demolition party of No. 3 Troop, were machine-gunned as they crossed the beach and lost some men before they gained the shelter of the cliff.

From the dubious cover of a ditch about 200 yards from the cliff edge, Captain Wills took stock of the situation. With less than 120 men instead of over 400, it was clear that the battery could not now be carried by assault, but if they could get within range it might be possible to prevent it from firing. Before they could move forward, a machine-gun in their front would have to be located and dealt with, so, taking two men, Captain Wills went off to the left and through the gardens of some villas to higher ground. From this vantage point they spotted the enemy gun, manned by two men. Borrowing a rifle, Captain Wills shot one and probably winged the other as he ran for his life. Now was the time to get the troops advancing, but as he turned to hurry back to his men, Captain Wills was hit in the neck. Seeing him fall, one of his companions, Corporal Halls, came back to help and was ordered to rejoin the main body and get them moving. After a period of unconsciousness, Captain Wills staggered back to the beach and eventually became a prisoner.

The Commandos pushed forward slowly against very

strong resistance. One party got into a building near the edge of the village, from which they were able to fire on the battery; others took cover in scattered houses and in a narrow lane running towards the village, and fought back savagely. By seven o'clock leading elements were more than 500 yards inland but unable to progress farther against very large numbers of German troops. Casualties had been heavy – the fields and roads were dotted with the bodies of dead and wounded Commandos – and the few surviving officers realized the position was hopeless. During the action it had been impossible to make any radio contact with their own H.Q. or with the Canadians, but by some fluke they were in direct communication with G.H.Q. in England. Earlier, Captain Wills had reported their precarious position and had been told to hold on, as Spitfires were being sent to give close support. So far they had not arrived, and shortly after seven o'clock it was decided to withdraw to the beach for evacuation. About this time the young American Ranger, Lt. Loustalot, attacking a machine-gun post single-handed, was killed within a few yards of it, while Corporal Halls rushed another post and killed the gunners with his tommy-gun.

The withdrawal was carried out skilfully to a bridge-head around the top of the gully, but when the first men reached the beach there were no landing-craft to take them off. One vessel was hard aground and burning, and another was apparently floating a little way out. A sergeant swam out to it under heavy fire, only to find a steel stake protruding through the craft's bottom, rendering it immobile.

Although the troops ashore were unaware of it, the five landing-craft had come in to attempt an evacuation. Closing the beach about seven o'clock, they found that the receding tide had exposed rows of steel spikes driven into the sand and extending some distance seawards. One craft impaled itself on a spike and could not get off; another, trying to avoid the suddenly revealed danger, ran ashore on the rocks and was stuck. The third succeeded in beaching and took on board the naval beach-party, and then, under a murderous fire from the cliffs, made valiant efforts to tow away the two grounded vessels, but was unable to move either of them. At this time there were no soldiers to be seen on the beach, and the craft withdrew. The two remaining landing-craft had been unable to get in, owing to the steel spikes and heavy enemy fire concentrated on the narrow channels between the rows. Reluctantly the three ships drew off, leaving Berneval beach to the quiet dead.

Ashore on the cliff top, in the lane, in ditches and in houses, the Commandos fought on, holding at bay at least four companies of German infantry, and not until ten o'clock did they surrender, by which time they were out of ammunition. The group in the building near the enemy battery held out until noon, in spite of being shelled by a nearby flak gun, and it seems that other little parties, out of touch with the main body, continued to fight long after the surrender.

Of the 120 men landed at Berneval, eighty, many of them wounded, were captured; the rest were dead. None got away.

While the prisoners were being removed in lorries, the belated Spitfires arrived and proceeded to shoot up the convoy of vehicles, causing further casualties to the battered Commandos.

Although the Yellow 1 landing has been written off as a failure, it is important to remember that the troops penetrated some way inland against very heavy opposition, and by drawing off the greater part of the large number of German reinforcements brought up, enabled Major Young's party to render the battery inoperative.

The Commandos' orders were, 'If you for any reason cannot overcome the battery, then you must remain and do your utmost to pin it down. It is of vital importance to the operation that this powerful battery does not fire during the initial stages of the attack on the main beach.'

As we have shown, the battery did not fire.

One of the few men to come off this beach alive and unwounded says, 'As we sailed in to Yellow Beach after the convoy battle, which gave us all a nasty few minutes and some casualties, everyone in my boat was very tense and keyed up. We had no idea where the rest of the ships had got to, but when we neared the shore, in full daylight, and saw it so quiet and deserted, we knew we were alone and in bad trouble. Expecting that the enemy would be sitting waiting for us, we were very surprised and relieved to land without a shot being fired at us. We made haste to get off the beach, but were held up while the wire was being cut. While this was being done, Jerry began firing from the cliffs, and although our passage through the wire was slow because of the mines, nobody, so far as I know, was hit, in spite of terrific firing overhead. Once on top, we went forward until we were stopped by very heavy machine-gun fire from the front. We were also being fired on from the left, so myself and three others crawled forward until we located the enemy position and gave it several bursts from our Stens. The firing stopped and we ran for a house just ahead, which we found empty. From the upper windows we had a good field of fire and saw a lot of Germans moving about. They went to ground quickly when we fired at them, and turned a machine-gun on us, smashing all the windows. We decided that two men would go out to outflank the gun, while the other two engaged it from the front. They soon came back to report too much open ground and too many Germans, so we thought we had better make our way back to the main body. We now noticed that the firing from our right, which had been very heavy all morning, had stopped except for occasional bursts. As we made towards the cliffs, we discovered a large party of Germans ahead of us, between us and the gully. It began to look as though we were cut off. We crawled up to the cliff edge and looked over, but could see no sign of our friends; the beach was deserted except for a burning vessel towards the west. I had the horrid thought that the troops had either pulled out or been overcome. In either event we were in a spot. Hiding among some bushes, we held a council of war and decided to make for Puys, where we knew the Canadians had landed, but to do so meant making a wide detour around the German battery which we had hoped to destroy.

'To our right in the direction of Puys the country was very open, and we could see many Germans moving about, so we reconnoitred towards the left where we found a sort of wooded valley leading to some wooded high ground. We came to a road on which there was a lot of military traffic heading towards Berneval, and after lying up for a long time managed to cross it and so reach the cover of the valley. From here we made our way to the woods. I knew there was a village somewhere ahead and there would surely be Germans. About then I realized the hopelessness of our position. We were moving away from the beach, the whole country seemed to be swarming with Germans, and the farther we went inland the less time we had to make the coast. From the south end of the wood we could see the village – and sure enough there were Germans. We held a council of war deep in the wood, and finally decided to lie up for a day or two until the excitement had died down, and then try to make the coast and find a boat – any sort of a boat in which to get back to England. We felt fairly safe in our hide-out, although we knew the enemy would be combing the whole area, and even dared to smoke. We stayed there the rest of the day, and all that night and part of the next day. By that time we were very hungry, but had plenty to drink from a stream close by. We would have to raid a house for food, even though the French would certainly tell the Germans. We knew they could get into bad trouble if they helped us, but perhaps we could steal some food without being seen. We found a farm-house on the east side of the wood, and one of the boys who could speak a little French approached. The place was dark and quiet, and we hoped the farmer and his family were away. Just as Jim was stealing across the yard, a dog rushed round the corner barking furiously, and as he skipped back to us the bloody dog followed, snapping at his heels and barking like hell. The door flew open and out popped a large-size farmer. We were caught, and putting a bold face on it, marched into the yard. When he saw we were English he began jabbering away and waving at us to get out. Jim asked for food but all he got was 'Non, Non, Non'. We pushed our way into the kitchen, and Jim asked for bread and meat. Nothing doing! Finally in exasperation I pointed my gun at him and snarled, 'Pan, biftek, vite' – about all the French I knew. It worked all right – his eyes popped and he pointed to a cupboard, where we found some long loaves and a hunk of what looked like horse. We grabbed these and beat it, feeling that our time was up. This unfriendly character would tell on us anyway, and we might as well surrender with full bellies. We retired to our wood and feasted. I never thought horse could taste so good.

'In the morning the place was full of Jerry patrols, and we decided to give ourselves up. We went back to the road, left our guns at the side, and set out slowly walking towards Berneval. The moment we saw any Germans we would wave our rather dirty handkerchiefs and put up our hands. By doing this we hoped to avoid being shot. Well, believe it or not, we must have walked two miles down that road without a sight of a Jerry. Twice Frenchmen on bicycles came along, took one goggle at us and fled like hell. They all seemed mortally afraid of what the Germans would do to them if they were seen talking to us. At last we heard a car and stood to one side with our hands up and our white flags waving. There were two German officers and a driver in the car. They screeched to a stop when they saw us, and the Jerries pulled out pistols and marched us down to the village. They treated us all right, gave us some grub and a cigarette and then drove us into Dieppe. For us the war was over, and only now did the full implication of it all strike me. After all those years of sweat and training which we had suffered, to end like this – the Troop destroyed, nothing achieved and myself a prisoner. Of course I was grateful to be alive, but although we tried to keep a bold face before the Germans, in secret we all suffered agonies of despair and frustration.'

Devastation

SHORTLY after 3 a.m., 252 men of No. 4 Commando Group, comprising A, B, C and F Troops, under Lt.-Col. Lord Lovat, were safely trans-shipped into their assault craft and set off on the final run-in to the Orange Beaches. At the head of the column a motor gunboat, commanded by Lt.-Commander Mulleneux, led the way. All was quiet, and the men, crowded in their little ships, were silent, their thoughts on what lay ahead. When the naval engagement on the eastern flank split the darkness with jagged flashes and the boom of artillery, one man said, 'Some poor so-and-sos are copping it out there.' But the men were not disturbed. It was none of their business and was comfortably far away.

It was as well for their peace of mind that they did not realize the reason for the sudden change of course made soon afterwards, as the leading ship sighted dead ahead the dark outlines of three enemy vessels creeping towards Dieppe. A quick alteration of course to starboard saved them, and the enemy ships vanished in the darkness, quite unaware of the convoy's presence. Regaining their correct course was simple, as in the distance they could see the flashes of the lighthouse on the Pointe D'Ailly, on either side of which they were to land. Three miles off shore the convoy split into two columns, that on the left, carrying C Troop, making for Orange 1, at Vaste-rival, just below Varengeville, and that on the right, with the rest of the force, heading for Orange 2 near Quiberville.

Their objective, the Hess battery and its surroundings, had been carefully studied with the aid of aerial photographs, and plans to deal with it formulated. The battery comprised six 15-cm naval guns, with a range of 23,000 yards, and its purpose was to engage enemy shipping in the waters off Dieppe. It was defended by two light dual-purpose ack-ack guns, an anti-tank gun and at least seven machine-gun posts, two in pillboxes and all enclosed in a strong wire perimeter fence which surrounded an area of some fifty acres. Through the centre of the battery site ran a road, from east to west, off which branched a lane immediately behind the guns, which were positioned towards the north or sea side of the perimeter, about 1,100 yards from the beach, Orange 1.

From this beach two precipitous gullies led upwards into a wood which continued to within 300 yards of the battery.

At the rear or south side of the perimeter there was another belt of woodland, with about the same width of open ground between it and the wire.

The plan of action was simple. C Troop, landing at Vasterival, would attack the battery from the front, while the rest of the force, landing about a mile to the west, would strike inland at top speed, and circling round in the shelter of the woods, come on the battery from the rear. At 6.20 cannon-firing fighter planes would launch an attack on the gun sites, and exactly at 6.30 the Commandos would begin their assault, from the south. C Troop would then withdraw, holding open a bridge-head at Vasterival beach until the main body had embarked.

The Hess battery was a tough proposition, but it was hoped that the holding attack on the front would keep the enemy engaged sufficiently to allow the wire at the rear to be breached and the main force to get into their jump-off positions. Every man had been thoroughly briefed and knew exactly what he had to do and where he had to go. It was an operation dear to their hearts and one in which speed and surprise were essential. It went completely right from the start.

As the two assault boats with C Troop approached Vasterival, the lighthouse on their right suddenly ceased to flash and a shower of star-shells shot up into the dark sky. It seemed that surprise had been lost, but the troops touched down at 4.45 a.m., dead on time, and landed without being fired on, only to find that both the exits from the beach were very heavily wired and impassable. There was nothing for it but to blow gaps in the wire at the risk of alarming the enemy, so the right-hand gully was chosen and two Bangalore torpedoes were exploded. By a stroke of luck, just then cannon fighters came in to shoot up the lighthouse, which was also the battery O.P., and the resulting clamour drowned the noise of the explosions. The men were quickly off the beach and setting about their various tasks – searching houses and the ground around the village, establishing a bridge-head on the cliffs above the gully, and one section moving off to cut the cable from the O.P. to the battery, being heavily fired on while doing so.

Led by Major Mills-Roberts, the main force advanced through the woods until they could both see and hear the German gunners, who were seemingly unperturbed by the firing from the cliff. The Commandos had with them a two-inch mortar, and this was set up and an observation post established at the edge of the wood. Every man selected a position from which he could fire direct into the battery, and at 5.40 the signal was given and C Troop opened fire. Unfortunately the mortar had been wrongly positioned and some time elapsed before it could enter the action. During the period when the troops had been moving to their positions, the battery had fired some intermittent salvoes, but now fell silent. Using snipers' rifles, Bren guns and an anti-tank rifle in addition to their usual weapons, the Commandos succeeded in knocking out the three machine-guns covering the front approach, and also picked off many of the gun crews. At 6.07 the mortar came into action and with its second shot hit one of the cordite dumps just behind the guns. This exploded with a great flash and roar, igniting other dumps and severely burning many of the unfortunate gunners. With the whole area around the guns ablaze, the greatest confusion reigned, men running about wildly, the screams of the burned gunners piercing the din of exploding ammunition, and lacing through the uproar the crump of the two-inch mortar bombs and the steady crackle of the Commandos' rifles as they poured their fire into the flames. As the blaze died away, the roar of aero-engines was heard and out of the sky came the Hurricanes, diving on the battery with cannons stuttering as they pressed home a low-level attack on the enemy position, and then at 6.30 the rockets signalling the readiness of Lovat's force were seen. Firing a last salvo of smoke-bombs over the battery, C Troop withdrew to the beach. So far they had suffered no casualties, but on the way

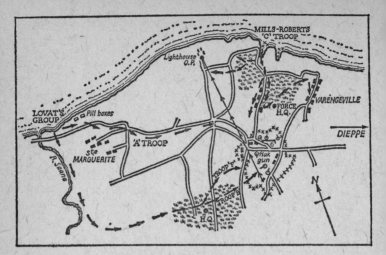

NO. 4 COMMANDO'S ATTACK ON HESS BATTERY

back a heavy mortar firing from somewhere to the east killed one man and wounded two.

Reaching the cliff top, C Troop took up defensive positions around the bridge-head perimeter, ready to receive a German counter-attack, but apart from occasional sniper-fire, there was no sign of the enemy. Soon Lovat's group were passing through the bridge-head to the beach, which was now under mortar and machine-gun fire, and at last C Troop followed them, wading out, like everyone else, up to their necks in the sea to the waiting vessels.

While C Troop were landing at Vasterival, the assault party of No. 4 Commando were coming ashore in the pre-dawn twilight on Ste Marguérite beach, west of the Phare D'Ailly. A Troop had been given the task of scaling the high cliffs and knocking out the two pillboxes covering the beach and the flat ground at the mouth of the River Saane, near which B and F Troop would make their landings at 4.50 a.m. Having accomplished this, they would then advance eastwards towards the battery to a pre-arranged position covering cross-roads along which enemy reinforcements from Ste Marguérite must proceed, thus sealing off the west flank of the main force. A Troop touched down on time, losing four men as they bridged the heavy wire. Using steel ladders, they quickly reached the cliff top, rushing the enemy posts before the Germans had a proper sight of them. At once star-shells shot up into the sky, and the morning quiet was shattered by the stutter of machine-guns and the crack of bursting grenades as the Commandos blasted the enemy from their pillboxes. In a few minutes it was all over and A Troop were racing for their objective.

Meanwhile, farther west, B and F Troops were struggling to cross the very heavy and thick wire which defended the low ground by the river mouth. Whilst doing so, they came under fire from mortars and machine-guns, suffering eight casualties, but it seemed that the enemy was unsure of his targets, for much of the fire was wild and misdirected. How-ever, no time was wasted on the dangerous beach, and five minutes after landing the whole force was over the wire and melting into the darkness of the country-side. It was a per-fect example of a Commando raid and left the enemy grasp-ing at empty air, with no means of knowing how many men had landed or where they had got to.

Once off the beach, the Commandos set off at the double along the east bank of the Saane and soon reached the wood-lands to the south of the battery. Here they separated, B Troop proceeding round the south side of the wood, while F Troop went by the north edge. While infiltrating through the trees, they heard with relish the explosion as the cordite in the battery blew up, a proof that all was well with their comrades on the far side of the gun site. Again the plan of action was simple. B Troop would assault some buildings on the right of the battery while F Troop went for the guns, but first both parties had to blow gaps in the wire and move forward over open ground to their jumping-off points. While B Troop were filtering through an orchard, they came under fire from a machine-gun post at the right-hand corner of the wire, but despite this a gap was blown in the wire, the ma-chine-gun was stalked and knocked out, and the men, under cover of smoke, quickly reached their start-line just short of the battery buildings. Here they lay down to await the signal for the final assault.

Things were tougher for F Troop, who had more open ground to cross before reaching the wire. Using smoke, they advanced down a road to the left or south-west corner of the perimeter, being heavily engaged by the enemy as they did so. There were a number of farm buildings just inside the wire at this point, and before they were cleared the troop commander was killed, a section officer mortally wounded and the troop sergeant-major also seriously wounded. A third officer, Captain Porteous, although himself wounded, took over, and fighting every inch of the way, F Troop finally reached their assembly positions in a ditch along the road immediately behind the gun emplacements. Both troops were now poised and ready for the onslaught on the main enemy positions. At precisely 6.20, the R.A.F. launched an attack by cannon-firing fighters on the guns, which went on for some minutes in spite of the efforts of German fighters to intercept the Hurricanes, and at 6.30 the signal for the assault was given.

Down came a dozen smoke-bombs from C Troop to shroud the whole battery position in drifting grey veils of fog, and in came the Commandos, charging with fixed bayonets across the bullet-swept open ground. Many men died in that mad rush, but there was no stopping the Commandos. With wild yells they were in among the guns and buildings, bayoneting, bombing and shooting the German gunners, who stubbornly defended their guns to the last. For a few minutes there was the wildest confusion in the vicinity of the buildings, with yelling Commandos chasing panic-stricken Germans in and out of the houses, some of which were already on fire. One German took refuge in a wooden shack, and, armed with a tommy-gun, defied all attempts to get him out. A grenade, fired through the window, sent the shack up in a sudden whoosh of flame. Out of the door burst a horrid blackened figure, with clothes afire and tommy-gun shooting, to run a few steps and then collapse as a merciful bullet ended his life.

Meanwhile, the demolition parties were busy at their work, blowing up the guns and destroying the buildings and stores. Once this was completed and the wounded carried back to the beach, the group withdrew, with A Troop acting as rear-guard. While the force were re-embarking from Vasterival beach, they came under desultory fire from the cliffs, but there were no further casualties and by eight o'clock they were afloat and away, taking with them four prisoners.

Ashore, the battery position was eerily quiet, the stillness broken only by an occasional crackle from a burning building or the moan of a wounded man. In an orderly row lay the bodies of twelve Commandos – two officers and ten men – who had fallen in the attack, and all round were the corpses of Germans – beside the wrecked guns, behind sand-bag breast-works, in the open ground – totalling, with wounded, not far short of one hundred. The Commandos lost, in addition to the twelve dead, twenty wounded, all of whom were brought home, and left behind another thirteen men, of whom nine were wounded but could not be found, and the remaining four dead.

Among the many heroes of the action mention must be made of Captain Porteous, who, although three times wounded, continued to lead and inspire his men to the very end. He was awarded the Victoria Cross, while one of the few American Rangers with the force, Corporal Koons, won a Military Medal, earning the distinction of being the first American to be thus honoured.

The success of this operation, in which about 250 Commandos assaulted a very strong position manned by an equal number of the enemy, was entirely due to the painstaking and thorough training of the troops involved. Under the supervision of Major D. Mills-Roberts, who was second-in-command of No. 4 Commando, and who led the group at Orange 1, the action had been practised and rehearsed for weeks beforehand. Every little detail had been worked out, even to the correct positioning of the men in the assault boats, to avoid delay in forming up on the beaches. Thanks to excellent navigation by the Navy, complete surprise was achieved, and the Commandos moved inland to their pre-arranged points without a hitch. The capture of this heavily defended battery by troops armed only with infantry weapons and a two-inch and three-inch mortar was a classic example of the use of highly trained infantry employing a carefully-thought-out and controlled fire plan. The action was to become a model for all future operations of the kind, and reflected the greatest credit upon Lord Lovat and Major Mills-Roberts, who saw their long months of arduous work brought to a triumphant conclusion. Both these men were very rightly decorated for their part in the affair, as were several officers and other ranks under their command.

Exploration

WHEN the first star-shells climbed into the sky above Quiberville, signalling the arrival of the Commandos on Orange 2, the men of Canada were fast approaching the inner beaches, from Pourville on the right to Puys on the left. The column nearest the shore was that carrying the South Sasks Regiment to Green Beach. On the left flank and still some miles out was the Royal Regiment of Canada, already late and moving at top speed in an effort to make up lost time. In the centre and still farther away, the Essex Scottish and R.H.L.I. were coming in steadily to their rendezvous on the Dieppe beaches. Packed tight in their assault boats were some 5,000 men of the 2nd Canadian Division: men from all walks of life and all parts of Canada – lumberjacks, miners, farm hands, bank clerks, mechanics, French-speaking trappers and factory workers from Quebec, all now knit together by a common purpose, one which was about to be realized and towards which they had been moving during all these past arduous months. On those dark and empty beaches ahead lay their destiny, and for many of them the future was only to be measured in minutes. In all that host there were very few men unmoved by the suspense of that long-drawn-out approach. Oppressed by the silence and darkness, with nerves tautened to breaking-point they waited. Soon that silence would be shattered by the menacing blasts of enemy gun-fire, and the blackness split by jagged tongues of flames as death reached out to them. With dry mouths they waited, while those who could, prayed.

While still about two miles out, the South Sasks heard, clear on the westerly breeze, the sound of firing away on their right. Someone said, 'It's started,' and a shiver of anticipation ran through the crowded ships. As they approached the coast the noise swelled in volume until they could distinguish the different weapons – the stutter of machine-guns, the thump of mortars, the bark of ack-ack guns, and forming a background to these individual notes, the growl of distant aircraft motors. Around them the silence was unbroken; ahead loomed the coast of France, dark and somehow ominous. They were on course and on time.

At five minutes to five o'clock the advance party of the South Sasks, under Lt. Mulholland, landed unopposed at Green Beach. Their task was to blow gaps in the wire with Bangalore torpedoes, and this they did, opening the way for A Company close behind. The explosions aroused the enemy, and some light machine-gun fire was directed at the beach while the company was landing, without causing any casualties. Hard on the heels of A Company came the rest of the regiment, but by now the enemy was alert and heavy machine-gun and mortar fire was encountered. So far the Germans seemed uncertain of what was taking place, and the fire was largely ineffective, but the South Sasks did not delay on the dangerous beach, and pushing forward rapidly, soon captured the village of Pourville. It was the intention to land two companies to the east of the River Scie, one to advance left-handed along the high ground to the radar station on the cliff edge, and the other to move inland to attack Quatre Vents Farm. The other two companies would be landed to the west of the river and would seize the village of Pourville and the high ground to the west. Through an error in navigation, the bulk of the four companies was landed west of the river and much of the advantage of the surprise landing was nullified. Now the two companies, A and D, whose objective was the radar station and the farm, had to force the crossing of the bridge over the Scie in face of very heavy machine-gun and mortar fire coming from the high ground to the east. The advance parties were killed or wounded, and the South Sasks were held up.

At this point the Commanding Officer, Lt.-Col. Merritt, having organized the defence of the village, appeared on the scene, and taking in the position at a glance coolly walked on to the bridge, waving his troops forward. Inspired by his courage, the men rushed across the bridge and immediately went into the attack on the farm and some gun positions which commanded the bridge and the beach. Meanwhile B Company was clearing Pourville of snipers, while C

Company had stormed an enemy strong-point to the west, but was unable to move farther as heavy fire was coming down on the position.

With great dash A Company overran two anti-tank guns and a machine-gun post, but their advance on the radar station was stopped by heavy and accurate cross-fire. D Company, reinforced by some elements of the Camerons, also could make no impression on Quatre Vents. Artillery support was essential, but alas, there was none. For a while it was hoped that the R.N.L.I., coming off Dieppe beach in an attack from the rear, would relieve the position, but as time went on and there was no sign of the expected attack, it was realized that the situation was rapidly deteriorating. All the South Sasks could hope to do was to hang on and endeavour to keep a line of retreat open for the Camerons, who were by now several miles inland. German reinforcements were coming up in large numbers and all positions were under heavy mortar fire. Outgunned and outnumbered, it was only a question of time before the defenders were driven back into the village and the whole extent of the beach laid open to the enemy guns.

At 9.30 a.m. a signal was received to prepare for withdrawal at ten o'clock, and a message to this effect was sent to the Camerons, from whom nothing had been heard since they set off inland three hours before.

The Cameron Highlanders of Canada made their landing at Pourville half an hour late, at 5.50 a.m., a delay caused by an error in navigation. Approaching the beach they came under heavy shell-fire, but none of the boats was hit and A Company, in the lead, got ashore with only a few casualties. The rest of the unit was not so fortunate, meeting a blast of machine-gun fire from a pillbox built into the cliffs on the left. Among those killed at the moment of touch-down was the Commanding Officer, Lt.-Col. Gostling, command reverting to Major Law.

Unfortunately the battalion was landed astride the River Scie, and most of D Company and the other companies' H.Q.'s found themselves on the east side of the river, when in fact they should have been on the west side. Major Law was quickly given the picture. Quatre Vents Farm had not yet been taken, and the bridge at Pourville was under heavy fire.

It was therefore decided to detour the Camerons along the west bank of the Scie, to Petit Appeville, and there across the river on their way to the rendezvous with the tanks near the Bois des Vertues.

No time was lost and the main body at once moved off, leaving those elements on the east side of the river to join with the South Sasks. With A Company in the lead, the Camerons advanced up the Pourville-Bas Hautot road, but coming under fire from Quatre Vents they swung to the right, seeking shelter of the woods. At a trail junction B and C Companies turned left towards Petit Appeville, while A Company secured the high ground on the right. From this vantage point the approaches from north, south and east were overlooked and a considerable amount of activity was observed on the roads. There was no sign of the tanks which by now should have been in the area, so it was decided to secure the bridge over the Scie and the high ground to the east of Petit Appeville, with the intention of advancing north to attack Quatre Vents from the rear.

Time was running out and it was realized that the attempt on the airfield must be abandoned. As the troops were moving off towards the bridge they had a brief encounter with two enemy patrols, and at the same time two 75-mm guns were observed being drawn into position to cover the approach to the bridge. A tempting target, but the Camerons had no weapon capable of reaching them at long range. The enemy were in increasing strength on the high ground covering the bridge and the Camerons were under constant machine-gun fire. Major Law thereupon ordered the withdrawal. As the troops were forming up, a message came from the South Sasks ordering them to return to Pourville for evacuation at ten o'clock. The time was 9.30, and the Camerons set off at once on their perilous journey. With C Company acting as rear-guard, fighting every inch of the way and suffering casualties, the battalion reached the village at ten o'clock, only to learn that the evacuation would not now begin until eleven o'clock, although an attempt would be made to get the wounded off at 10.30. The South Sasks had been driven back from the high ground east and west of the town, and the Camerons at once launched a counter-attack uphill to the west. They regained some ground, but it was a short-lived respite. The enemy came

75

back with mortars and machine-guns in overwhelming numbers, causing heavy casualties to the Canadians and gradually forcing them back into the village. By 10.30, when the first landing-craft appeared, the enemy had possession of all the high ground at both ends of the beach. Now the slow agony of the evacuation began. In addition to the high-water beach, some 200 yards of shallows left by the ebbing tide had to be traversed before the precarious shelter of the ships could be reached, and all in full sight of the German gunners. First came the wounded, carried on stretchers by the devoted men of the R.C.A.M.C., some supported by their comrades, staggering, crawling, hopping – long lines of men struggling through an inferno of flame and smoke and flying steel. For many of them their sufferings on that nightmare journey were in vain – they died even as they stretched out their hands to the promise of succour; others, mortally wounded, fell back into the sea and, their mouths full of salt water, choking, coughing, fought to regain the land before they drowned.

Time after time the stretcher-bearers returned to pick up all who could be moved, until at last it was done and the beach was empty except for the dead. During this time several motor boats, recklessly sailing close inshore, had been pounding the German positions with their light weapons, and now they were joined by the destroyers, putting up a furious bombardment of the high ground to the west, where the heaviest fire was coming from. Protected to some extent by this barrage, the landing-craft came in once more, and using the last of their smoke-canisters to cover them, the South Sasks and Camerons began to embark. The prospect of braving that open stretch of beach was one to daunt the bravest, but in good order and discipline they moved down through the fog and into the shallow water. The enemy, seeing his prey slipping through his fingers, brought every available weapon to bear, firing blindly through the mist and turning the half-mile of beach into a mad whirl of exploding shells and screaming tracer. Then came the Stukas, diving down from the clouds, machine-gunning and bombing the landing-craft and the beach. It seemed that nothing could live under such an intense bombardment, but still men came out climbing aboard the ships, until by twelve o'clock every vessel was packed to capacity and backing off that deadly

76

shore. As they went astern and began to turn away, the sea leapt up around them in great spouts as the enemy guns pursued them. One craft, receiving a direct hit in the bows, sank immediately, leaving wounded and unwounded men struggling in the water, some to be picked up, others to die from the hail of bullets lashing the sea into foam around them. A few managed to reach the shore, exhausted from swimming in heavy clothes against the outgoing tide.

The smoke had now cleared from the foreshore, where many men were patiently waiting for rescue. In Pourville the rear-guard fought on doggedly in face of ever-growing enemy pressure. One last effort would have to be made to get these men away before it was too late.

About 12.30 two landing-craft attempted to close the beach, but were driven off by an intense artillery barrage. It seemed a hopeless prospect with no smoke-cover, and there were no more smoke-bombs. As a desperate expedient it was decided to set the houses on the sea front alight, in the hope that the resulting smoke would provide sufficient cover for the rear-guard to make a dash for the beach. But all the available incendiaries were defective, and the houses not of a type to burn easily. The landing-craft, standing off, looked in vain for the expected smoke. None came, and when a signal from the shore reported the position, it was realized that all hope of saving the men had gone. None the less, the Navy were reluctant to give up, and several vessels made a gallant attempt to approach the beach, but were driven off in spite of most determined efforts to get in. Only when they were all hit and badly damaged did they turn away.

Over 200 men were still in Pourville, and once it became clear that all hope of rescue had gone, they settled down to fight it out, holding on until all ammunition was exhausted and they were captured.

Of some 500 Camerons who landed 270 got away, and many of them were wounded. The South Sasks casualties were equally high. Amongst the dead on Pourville beach was found the body of a French youth who had tried to escape in one of the landing-craft, and near by were the corpses of three Germans, prisoners who had swum ashore when the vessel they were in was sunk. They reached the shore only to die by their own guns.

One of the many heroes of that memorable day was

Corporal H. C. Keys, of D Company, South Sasks, whose courage and leadership earned him the D.C.M. Having attacked the enemy in a most determined fashion throughout the action, he brought his section back to the beach for embarkation. At this time the beach was being subjected to heavy artillery and mortar fire, in addition to small-arms fire, but Corporal Keys, entirely voluntarily, climbed to a commanding position and engaged the enemy with a machine-gun. He remained in this most exposed part of the beach for some twenty minutes, until, in the words of the official citation, 'he was hit and literally hurled from the top of the groyne'. Badly wounded, he refused to allow his comrades to carry him to the landing-craft, and was taken prisoner. He returned to Canada in 1945, and in 1946 was presented with his well-deserved decoration.

Corporal Key's conduct was typical of the fighting spirit of the Canadians, both at Pourville and elsewhere. Hear a private of the Camerons, who was wounded by a mortar shell the moment he landed on the beach:

'There I was fifty yards away from the sea-wall, both legs full of holes – the machine-guns were traversing the shore line and mortars laying down a barrage. I dug myself in, in about two seconds. After about an hour I made it to the sea wall. The feeling was returning to my legs and I found that they were still serviceable, more painful than serious. An officer got a few walking wounded to lay a covering fire on a pillbox on the West Headland. I found a mortar and a few smoke-bombs, and kept it blanketed until I ran out of bombs. Later we went into the village to clear out snipers, and got a few. We all knew we were in a bad spot, but I didn't see anyone who seemed to be worrying about it. We did a bit of sniping on our own. I made the best shot of my life at a running Jerry on the East Headland, and tagged him with a snap shot at 300 yards. Later the word came round that we were to evacuate. I got to the beach just as the last boat-load of wounded pulled out. About 11 a.m. another flight came in, and I set a record for the 100 yards' dash making for the nearest. I collected two more hits on the way, one in the arm and the other in the jaw, but I made the boat. When we were out 200 yards, our bow was blown off and the boat sank at once. My Mae West was punctured and it was hard work getting ashore against the tide. I got back to the wall, although the beach was fairly humming with bullets. I was ordered to rejoin my company near the bridge, and found the boys in their usual frame of mind betting on the outcome and not too perturbed at their predicament. Soon afterwards we were ordered back to the beach, but when we got there found that the last boat had left. Colonel Merritt, of the South Sasks, got us organized and we continued to resist until we ran out of ammo.

'We sent out one of our prisoners with a white flag, and in a few moments German soldiers appeared on the sea wall and brought us up on to the street. We were herded into a short street with high brick walls, about 150 of us, and while there were strafed by a flight of Spitfires, but only one man was hit in the leg. In the evening we were marched into the hospital in Dieppe, where the sisters were very kind to us. We then had to march inland to Envermu, where we spent the night in a ruined factory.'

Three times wounded, thrown back on the beach from the threshold of safety, he returns to the fight undaunted, and with his comrades cheerfully faces the prospect of death or confinement. He was just one of that splendid band of young men, all permeated with the determination to give a good account of themselves, come what may. Is it any wonder the German troops returning from Pourville were dispirited and downcast? The British had landed, in spite of what Hitler had said, 'and if these are the sort of troops they have, God help us!' This remark was passed by a disillusioned German to a Frenchman, and represented the feelings of the Germans engaged in the fight for Pourville.

Annihilation

At about the time the South Sasks were making their successful landing at Pourville, part of the flotilla carrying the Royal Regiment of Canada was creeping along the coast, seeking the narrow entrance to Puys beach. Delayed at the trans-shipment point by the temporary loss of their escort, they had been badly shaken by the naval battle on their left, which was too close for comfort. Aircraft had been heard overhead and flares had been dropped, so that they felt all security had gone.

Now as they drew near the shore, a searchlight blazed out, lighting up the sea for miles, and every man knew they could no longer count upon taking the enemy by surprise. It was a grim prospect, but somehow no one thought of turning back – all knew it was vital to the success of the whole enterprise that they should get ashore and overrun the East Headland from the rear.

Men braced themselves for the fiery ordeal they knew awaited them on the small beach now visible in the grey light of dawn. They had not long to wait. While still some hundreds of yards off shore, they came under rifle and machine-gun fire, and some men in the leading craft were hit. But this was but a foretaste of what was to come. As the craft touched down and dropped their ramps, and the Royal poured out on to the 200-yard beach, they were met by an appalling burst of machine-gun fire, coming from both flanking cliffs and from the sea wall ahead. The time was seven minutes past five o'clock. They were twenty minutes late.

In an instant the narrow beach becomes a death-trap. Many men are killed even before they can leave the ships; those behind, stumbling over the bodies of their comrades, are shot down as they reach the beach. Others, who by some miracle are as yet untouched, burrow in the loose shingle seeking what precarious shelter they can find, while around and over them the air whistles and whines with flying bullets, and mortar-bombs erupt in black smoke along the beach.

In a few short minutes the first wave of the Royal Regiment has been cut to pieces, the survivors pinned down and helpless on the stones.

In some of the landing-craft little groups of men, shocked and stunned by the brutal, violent and sudden death all around them, huddle together staring with horror at the bodies of their comrades in the water and on the beach. This is not what they have been told to expect – this is not the quick dash across the foreshore and on to a sleeping enemy. This is sheer murder, landing in daylight under a ferocious fire from all sides. With minds frozen by the sudden awful realization of what they have to do, they crowd away from the gaping mouths of the craft until the naval officers, anxious to get off the deadly beach, intervene and succeed in restoring order and discipline.

Puys beach has a sea wall about ten feet high, with buttresses on the seaward side. The top of the wall was protected by heavy coils of barbed wire, and somehow some men who had reached the wall managed to climb up and with Bangalore torpedoes blow gaps in the wire. Covered by fire from their comrades on the beach, a few men struggled through these gaps, in a brave attempt to reach the east cliff and attack a house and pillbox from which heavy fire was enfilading the beach. Their bodies were afterwards found in the wire and on the cliff top before the house.

At the western end of the beach a small party, under the Commanding Officer, Lt.-Col Catto, managed with great difficulty to cut their way through the wire and gain the cliff top. There they attacked two houses from which heavy fire was coming, killed the occupants and destroyed the guns. Attempting to return to the beach, they found the gap in the wire under intense fire and enemy patrols advancing to cut them off. It seemed their only chance was to move westward in the hope of reaching Dieppe, but the whole area of the East Hill was infested by enemy patrols, and there was no way down to the beach. They hid in a wood for some hours, and there they were discovered and captured.

Meanwhile, on Puys beach a succession of tragedies was

being played out. At about 5.30 a.m. the second wave of landing-craft came in and under heavy shell-fire approached the beach, now barely discernible through the smoke being laid down by the R.A.F. One landing-craft lowered its ramp before touching down, leaving the men exposed to the very heavy machine-gun fire coming down on the verge of the sea. Private J. Poolton, of D Company, who were put ashore near the eastern end of the beach, tells his story of those tragic moments. He was in the craft which dropped its ramp prematurely, and, carrying a two-inch mortar, stepped off into eight feet of water.

'When I hit the water I dropped the mortar and bent down, completely submerged, to retrieve it. I was carrying the mortar, twelve bombs, two hand-grenades and 200 rounds of .303 ammunition in addition to my rifle, and waded ashore under water until I reached the land. Someone shouted at me to run, but with that load I could barely drag myself to the wall. Bullets were kicking up the stones at my feet, but I was not hit. Under the wall I found the mortar would not fire because of its immersion in the sea. I noticed that the men carrying the '18' sets [radio], Bren guns and three-inch mortars were picked off by snipers. I saw one signaller trying desperately to contact the H.Q. ship, but evidently he was not being received. We tried to signal the destroyer to put down fire on the wall, but our signals were not seen as the destroyer was under fire from the shore batteries and was being attacked by aircraft. We kept firing at the house to our left from which heavy machine-gun fire was coming, but soon realized our position was hopeless. There was just a chance that the tanks which we knew had gone ashore at Dieppe might come to our rescue, but as time went on and the German fire seemed to get worse, we knew we were done for.'

Shortly after the landing of the second wave, some vessels bearing the Black Watch of Canada and some detachments of artillerymen approached. The officer in charge quickly spotted that the heaviest fire was coming from the cliffs on the left, and directed that the troops be landed at the western end of the beach. The landing was effected without casualties, but the men were unable to move and were eventually captured. Their role was to capture and man the enemy guns in the vicinity, a task which of course was impossible.

About 6.30 a.m. a lone landing-craft came in under a hail of fire. Delayed on the run-in by engine failure, she was bringing the last of the Royal Regiment to their appointment with death. Steadily she approached, the shell-torn sea leaping in great spouts around her, touched down, lowered her ramp and then, half hidden by flying spray, backed off without putting any of her people ashore. On the beach and under the wall the survivors of the 550-strong battalion crouched among the corpses of their comrades. Leaderless and disorganized, they lay huddled on the blood-stained shingle, searching the sea for the ships they felt sure would come for them. To move was to court death from the enemy watching and waiting around that dreadful arena. To simulate death was the only way to live.

Nothing was known aboard the H.Q. ship of the plight of the Royal Regiment. About 6.40 a.m. a message was received saying that the Regiment had failed to land, but this was quickly followed by the arrival in person of the naval flotilla leader to report that the landing had been carried out successfully. Since then there had been no news until, at 7.30 a.m., a signal came from Blue Beach asking to be taken off. This request caused considerable puzzlement to those on H.M.S. *Calpe*, who ascribed it to German sources. However, a motor-boat and some landing-craft were eventually sent to Puys to attempt an evacuation. The ships met intense shell-fire and only one landing-craft reached the beach. She was already badly holed, and, overwhelmed by the rush of men who scrambled aboard, sank as she pulled off into deep water. A few of the struggling survivors were picked up, the only men of the Royal Regiment to come off Blue Beach, apart from those in the landing-craft mentioned above, which did not land her complement. Several further attempts were made to close the beach, but in vain.

Each time the vessels were discerned approaching, a concentration of shell-fire was brought down on them from the heavy battery behind Puys and from dual-purpose anti-aircraft guns. To penetrate that barrage was suicide, and reluctantly all further endeavours were abandoned. German records show that the four-gun battery at Puys fired no less than 550 shells that morning. This in addition to an uncounted number of missiles from ack-ack guns and mortars.

Three times the enemy called upon the Royals to surrender on pain of being wiped out, and at the third call, realizing the hopelessness of the position, they gave in. The Germans quickly hustled all who could walk off the beach to the village, leaving most of the badly wounded where they lay. Later they permitted some of the Royals to return to the beach and carry off some of the wounded, but with the appearance of landing-craft off shore this was stopped, and many wounded men remained there all day until finally picked up by the Germans. By this time a number had died from loss of blood and from exhaustion. This seemingly callous behaviour maddened the French villagers and the prisoners, but in extenuation let it be said that the Germans expected a further landing attempt at Puys. The appearance of vessels off the beach on several occasions convinced them that reinforcements were in the offing.

This murderous action cost the Royal Regiment no less than 227 dead, while 264 men were taken prisoner, of which 103 were wounded. Only sixty-five men came back to England, of which number sixty-two had not been landed. The high proportion of dead can only be attributed to the smallness of the battlefield, where wounded men were hit again as they lay in the open, and to some extent to the failure of the Germans to remove the wounded after the surrender.

The Black Watch and artillery units escaped with slight casualties, thanks to the quick thinking of the officer in command, but all who were put ashore became prisoners.

Relative to the dearth of information about Blue Beach received by the H.Q. ship, one strange fact came to light. It seems that the forward observation officer of H.M.S. *Garth* was ashore at the western end of the beach and in continuous wireless communication with his vessel. Many messages from him reporting that the force was held up were received by *Garth* and duly passed to *Calpe*, but were apparently not received by the H.Q. ship. The Army signallers ashore, who one by one fell victims to German snipers, had also been unable to make contact with *Calpe*, the only signal to get through being the one at 7.30 a.m. which was viewed with such suspicion at H.Q. This was almost certainly authentic, and after it nothing more was heard from Blue Beach.

Revelation

Dieppe, Red and White Beaches

In the last half-hour before dawn the troops destined for the Dieppe beaches were sailing in, dead on time. All had gone well with their trans-shipment, and now the men were keyed up and taut with expectation as zero hour remorselessly approached.

In the lead were, on the left, the Essex Scottish Regiment heading for the Red Beach, near the harbour wall, and on the right, the Royal Hamilton Light Infantry, who would land on White Beach, close to the West Headland, Hindenburg. With them were the sappers of the Royal Canadian Engineers, whose task it was to breach the wire entanglements on the beach.

Farther back were ships with mortar detachments of the Black Watch of Canada, who soon would turn away to port and set course for Puys, where they were to land in support of the Royal Regiment. To starboard of the Black Watch were the support landing-craft, bristling with machine-guns manned by the Toronto Scottish. Their job was to lie in close to the beach and give covering fire to the troops ashore.

Behind the assault groups came the tank landing-craft, with sixty Churchill tanks manned by men of the Calgary Regiment. The tanks would land in successive waves, the first nine with the infantry at 5.20. Away out at sea, moving slowly, were the vessels carrying the floating reserve, comprising the Fusiliers Mont Royal and the Royal Marine 'A' Commando, the latter with their special task of seizing the harbour and any ships therein.

All this vast concourse of little ships was escorted by numerous motor gunboats and launches, with the eight destroyers prowling on their flank. Zero hour was 5.20 a.m., and shortly before five o'clock, fine on their starboard bows, the dark sky was lit by gun flashes and flares as the first landings went in on the right. Faintly at first, then growing in volume, the roar of battle came booming across the calm sea and soon was swelled by a crackling thunder from the left, as the Royal Regiment went to their doom at Puys.

So, with the harsh noise of war in their ears, the main assault force drew near their rendezvous, now clearly outlined against the greying sky but still dark and quiet. To the outward eye Dieppe was wrapped in slumber, undisturbed by the clamour of the guns on either side, but the approaching troops knew that behind that darkness watchful eyes were scanning the dim expanse of water for signs of hostile craft. Wakeful men were there on those black cliffs manning a variety of weapons, expectant of the order that would transform the pre-dawn hush into hellish, deadly uproar.

The sea front at Dieppe, running from the harbour wall in the east to the headland in the west, is almost a mile long. At high tide the beach varies in width from 200 yards to 350 yards, and is composed of shingle stones, sloping in a series of folds or steps down to sand which is uncovered at low tide. Behind the beach is a concrete sea wall about four feet high, with a promenade and the maritime boulevard, called Boulevard Maréchal Foch. Beyond the Boulevard Foch are lawns and gardens, 150 yards in depth and running the whole length of the front. On the landward side of the gardens is the Boulevard Verdun, parallel to the sea and lined with hotels and boarding-houses. Slightly to the left of centre were two tall chimneys of the tobacco factory, and on the extreme right, overlooking the beach and under the West Headland, was the Casino with its high tower. Intersecting the Boulevard Verdun and giving access to the town are fourteen streets from the Rue de Sygogne on the right to the Quai de Hoble on the left, beside the base of the harbour wall.

Aerial photographs and Intelligence reports had revealed that concrete walls with firing positions had been erected across the entrances to all these streets. The gardens were full of rifle-pits and trenches, artillery observation posts had been noticed on the Promenade, and heavy wire defences stretched the full length of the beach. The West Headland was known to have many machine-gun positions covering the beach, some in caves dug into the sides of the cliffs. Field-guns had been detected on the terrace of the castle on the West Headland, and there were pillboxes beside the Casino and what appeared to be gun emplacements, although no guns were seen. The Casino building itself did not appear to have been fortified, at least no sand-bags or blocked-up windows were apparent, but there would undoubtedly be machine-guns there. The hotels on the sea front contained both artillery and machine-guns, and finally the East Hill, slightly behind the docks and commanding the beach, was likely to be well armed. It was thought that machine-guns had been installed in the natural caves in these cliffs, in addition to observed gun-positions on the top. There were a large number of anti-aircraft guns in the area, some of which could be used for beach defence, and nine small-calibre anti-tank guns, most of which had not been detected, including two which appeared at the Casino during the night and were withdrawn at first light. On the harbour wall were two more anti-tank guns, one in a pillbox near the lighthouse and the other in a tank which had been walled in at the base of the pier. There were also no less than eight French 75-mm. guns for beach defence, some on the West Headland and the majority in the caves of the East Headland. The presence of these guns was entirely unsuspected by the British. On either side of Dieppe were four batteries of ten-centimetre field-guns, comprising sixteen guns in all, as well as the heavy coastal batteries already mentioned, all of which had been carefully reconnoitred from the air. This, then, was the fortress of Dieppe, approached with such high hopes by some 2,000 highly-trained Canadians in the dark of the early morning of 19th August.

While the leading assault craft were about a mile off shore, a thunder of gun-fire from seaward marked the opening of the naval covering bombardment, and at ten minutes past five o'clock the distant grumble of aero-engines grew to a roar, as waves of bombers and fighters swept in to attack the hotels lining the front. At once the beach and gardens became an inferno of exploding shells and bombs, while overhead the sky was filled with ack-ack bursts and ribbons of orange tracer. Men in a landing-craft cannot see ahead or to either side, they can only see upwards, and the Canadians stared in fascination at the display of deadly pyrotechnics above them. Some tracer was seen floating lazily, seemingly harmless, just above their heads, and a succession of clangs on the steel side of the ships brought home to them with a sudden shock that they were under fire. But there was no time to dwell on it. The men swayed as the ships grated on the shingle, the ramps crashed down, and surging forward they got their first glimpse of Dieppe – grey stones and monstrous coils of wire. For many of them their first glimpse is their last, as with a stunning explosion of sound the German guns roar out. It is 5.23 a.m. They are three minutes late. Spread out along the beach, half hidden by smoke, the landing-craft and the men leaping from them are swept by a murderous hail of steel. From the West Hill, from the Casino, from the Harbour wall and from dozens of well-concealed positions, heavy M.G.s, anti-tank guns and high-velocity field-guns spout forth death upon the men struggling to gain a foothold on the beach. D Company of the R.H.L.I., coming ashore near the Casino, are practically wiped out in the first minute. The small groups of sappers struggling to reach the wire are all killed or wounded at the moment of landing. Behind them the main force, charging from the assault craft over the bodies of their comrades, die in scores on the verge of the sea. The Official Canadian History, quoting battle reports, mentions that the fire from the shore appeared to slacken somewhat just before touch-down; this may have been the result of the really terrifying aerial attack, which ended exactly as planned at 5.25. If this was indeed so – and not everyone agrees that it was – then the loss of those precious three minutes in landing made all the difference between success and failure. One man, describing that moment of truth when first he set foot on the enemy shore, said, 'It was like walking out into a huge swarm of bees, the lead was so thick you could see it coming and going in all directions.' However, many men survived that first fearful blast of fire, and somehow they reached the comparative safety of the sea wall. Here, confused and shaken by the unimagined ferocity of their reception, they crouch, while the few surviving officers strive to make some semblance of order out of chaos. Behind them the beach is littered with the bodies of their comrades, the wounded, the dying and the dead. Here and there men, so far unharmed, scrabble at the shingle as they seek shelter from the storm that beats about them. The few mortar crews and machine-gunners who reach the beach are special targets as they struggle to set up their weapons at the water's edge. Some succeed in getting off a few rounds against the unseen enemy, only to be obliterated by a barrage of shells brought down upon them by the watchful observation post on the Promenade. In those first few minutes every man still alive knew the bitter truth – the attack had failed; they were in a trap. The tanks which should have landed with them and given close support during the most dangerous moments of the assault had not appeared. Through an error in navigation the three carriers with nine tanks aboard had got off course, and were fifteen minutes late. Now at 5.35 they came in, closely followed by the three carriers of the second wave, and as the vessels emerged from the smoke they were blasted by a concentrated fire from the anti-tank guns placed on the Promenade. Immediately they were in difficulties, some with their ramps shot away, others with their steer-ing-gear smashed, all reeling beneath the impact of heavy shells and fighting desperately to get in and land their burdens.

The tank landing-craft carried, in addition to tanks, de-tachments of the Royal Canadian Engineers and of the Toronto Scottish Machine-Gunners, the latter to go ashore to support the infantry. As defence against aircraft the vessels had been fitted with two heavy machine-guns on high-angle mountings, manned by other parties of the Toronto Scottish, amongst whom were Corporal Ferguson and Private Page. They had spent most of the night hauling heavy tank-blocks up from below to build a barricade round their machine-gun on the exposed bow of the ship, and now as they approached the shore the vessel was struck again and again by shells and flayed by machine-guns. About 200 yards out, a direct hit in the motor-room left them without power, and as the T.L.C. drifted slowly towards the beach a shell burst on the bow, blowing overboard the machine-gun and most of the bar-ricade, wounding Page and leaving Ferguson lying dazed on the deck. As he struggled to collect his senses, he heard the shouts of a party of the Essex Scottish as they charged down the ramp, closely followed by the three tanks, which, with motors roaring, splashed into the shallows and clambered up the beach. But they, like many of the other tanks now scattered along the shore, cannot gain traction on the steep, shifting shingle. Floundering and swerving, they dig deep grooves in the stones while shells fired at close range smash against their armour. Some belly down in the treacherous shingle, while others come to rest with broken tracks. A few, favoured with better luck or better grip, keep moving forward. Slowly they lumber up the beach, smash through the wire and so to the wall. Here, rearing up, their guns pointing skywards, they pull themselves on to the Promenade and set off down the Boulevard Foch, engaging the enemy guns in the hotels and pillboxes. Their immediate aim is to get off the Promenade and into the town, but this is impossible. Tank-traps and strong concrete walls bar the way and prove impervious to the tanks' guns. The sappers who had come in with the tanks and whose job it was to demolish those obstacles are either dead or pinned down at the verge of the sea. The tanks are trapped in the open, targets for the anti-tank guns firing from the hotels and from behind the concrete barriers. Some return to the beach, others roar up and down the boulevards desperately seeking to escape from the massive fire directed upon them from a score of points. All, sooner or later, are immobilized, in the Gardens or on the beach, with broken tracks or damaged turrets. But they are not yet out of the fight. Until their last round is fired they spit defiance at the enemy. The tank crews, helpless and frustrated, are quick to find that the enemy fire in general cannot 'brew them up', and so long as they remain inside they are comparatively safe. Only the 75s could hope to penetrate the heavy armour of the Churchills, and the 75s are, for the moment, silent, hidden behind a blanket of impenetrable fog. Of the eighteen tanks landed in the first waves, only eight are known to have got off the beach. None entered the town. Meanwhile the T.L.C. with Corporal Ferguson aboard, had been badly damaged by shell-fire as she lay broadside to the shore. Another T.L.C. took her in tow, but she sank immediately in deep water, Ferguson being lucky to be picked up and brought back unharmed to England. Page, wounded as he was, swam ashore from the sinking craft and became a prisoner. Of the six tank landing-craft in the first two flights, four were left, smashed and riddled on the beach or in the deep water just off it.

Shortly after six o'clock the smoke over the East Headland cleared, and as it did so the third wave of tanks was observed closing the beach in four landing-craft. At once they became the centre of a vortex of fire, as the 75s, so long frustrated, entered the fray. In a few moments all four vessels were in a sinking condition, torn and rent by the heavy armour-piercing projectiles, many of their crews dead or dying. With unaccustomed hands at the helms, they fought their way in to the beach to discharge their precious cargoes. One tank dropped off into deep water and was drowned. This was the vehicle carrying the Commanding Officer, Lt.-Col. Andrews. He and the crew scrambled out and reached the shore, but were shot down at the water's edge. Of the remainder, one stalled its motor while still aboard the craft and could not restart, but the other ten gained the beach, and seven of them were reported as having crossed the wall to join their fellows in the death struggle taking place in the Pleasure Gardens. In all, twenty-nine tanks out of thirty in the first three waves were put ashore, and of this number fifteen or maybe sixteen crossed the wall. As we have shown, it was impossible to enter the town because of the concrete barriers, and many of these tanks returned to the beach and continued the fight from there. Aerial photographs taken by the R.A.F. showed five tanks on the lawns, and this led to the erroneous assumption that these were the only tanks to have crossed the wall. The tank crews remained in their vehicles fighting to the last, and this contributed to the smallness of the fatal casualties suffered by them – only thirteen killed out of a total of some 170 men put ashore. Unfortunately their rear-guard action meant that all the rest were taken prisoners – all, that is, except one lucky individual who managed to get aboard one of the landing-craft.

Out at sea the tanks of the 4th Group awaited the order to go in. All that long morning they waited, under air-attack and constant shelling, fearful of being sunk and eager to get ashore to join their comrades in whatever fate awaited them. But the order was never given, and shortly after nine o'clock the tank landing-craft set out on their return journey to England. There were many sore hearts amongst the tank crews as they thought of their friends left behind. What had happened to them they did not know and might never know. Later that evening a German aircraft came screaming over the little town of Seaford, where the Tank Regiment was stationed, and dropped bundles of photographs taken that same day. These pictures were of groups of prisoners, and enabled the tank men to identify many of their comrades as being still alive. The bundles were dropped dead in the centre of the parade ground, which everyone had thought to be well camouflaged.

The men of the Royal Canadian Engineers, some of whom had come in with the infantry in the assault boats with the object of blowing gaps in the wire, and some landing with the tanks to demolish anti-tank barriers, suffered heavily in the first few minutes. A few parties were unable to get ashore, as the T.L.C.s in which they were carried pulled back off the beach immediately the tanks were landed, and were prevented from touching down again by damage to the ramps. Those men who did reach the beach and survived found themselves pinned down, their equipment lost or damaged by fire. Anything lying about the beach became the target for machine-gunners and snipers using a high proportion of tracer, which set alight anything of an inflammable nature. Some did succeed in reaching the shelter of the wall and the Casino, and several made determined efforts to cross the bullet-swept Gardens and so reach the tank barriers, only to be shot down. One at least managed to place a charge against the tank barrier near the Casino, but it was unexploded and was noticed there the following day by a Frenchman.

It is impossible to state accurately the number of Royal Canadian Engineers who actually set foot on Dieppe beach, but out of seven officers and 309 other ranks who embarked in England, six officers and 182 other ranks became casualties either killed, wounded or prisoners.

The Toronto Scottish Machine-Gunners fared better. Out of 125 men embarked, only one soldier was killed, four were taken prisoner and 120 returned, of whom eight were wounded. Many of the machine-gunners were on the T.L.C.s which did not land their tanks and which were sent home early in the action, which doubtless accounts for the small casualty-list.

Meanwhile, on Red and White Beaches, the remnants of the two assaulting battalions are fighting for their lives. Huddled under the sea wall or crouching in hollows scooped out of the shingle, they fire their rifles and Brens at the well-entrenched and invisible enemy. With the failure of the tanks the first momentum of the assault was lost, but many men were not content to play a passive role. On the left, a group of the Essex Scottish, led by C.S.M. Stapleton, taking advantage of smoke-cover, crossed the deadly expanse of Promenade and Gardens, and working their way around behind the Boulevard de Verdun, entered some of the houses and cleared them of the enemy. They penetrated as far as the harbour and are reported to have accounted for a number of enemy snipers and men in transport. Most of the little party were eventually captured, but C.S.M. Stapleton got back to the beach, and in due course was awarded the D.C.M.

Three more attempts were made by the Essex Scottish to attack through the Gardens, but all were beaten back by very heavy fire, and by six o'clock it was clear to the surviving officers that any further organized advance was impossible. Although many of the houses on the Boulevard de Verdun were burning, machine-gun and mortar fire continued to pour out from the buildings in front, as well as from pill-boxes and trenches in the Gardens. In addition, the battalion was under fire from the harbour wall on the left flank, where the Germans had dug in a French tank. Fighting grimly, the Essex Scottish settled down beneath the sea wall to wait.

On White Beach conditions were no better. With the guns of the West Headland firing straight down on to the beach, the Royal Hamilton Light Infantry were trapped, but here there was some hope of advancing if the Casino could be taken. This building was full of Germans who were sniping and firing machine-guns from the windows overlooking the beach. In addition, two pillboxes at each end covered the gun-emplacements, where two anti-tank guns were in position. Covered by a short bombardment from the sea, an attack on the building was launched. After some fierce fighting the R.H.L.I. broke into the lower part, and aided by some men of the Royal Canadian Engineers, blew up the

93

pillboxes and the two guns. While the fighting was still raging in and around the Casino, a party led by Captain Hill entered the building, and running across the forecourt gained the houses at the western end of the Boulevard de Verdun. Here they broke into a house which let them through to a theatre, from which they got into the town. Some of this party penetrated as far as the church of St. Rémy, in which Brigade H.Q. were to have been established, but finding no one there, withdrew to the theatre, where they held out against German attacks until ten o'clock, when they returned to the Casino. While in the theatre they were joined by a party of sappers led by Sergeant Hickson, who brought his men through the streets, destroying telephone wires and electric installations and engaging the enemy whenever he appeared. This group also got back to the beach, although not without losses.

It is possible that another party got into the town in this area, as French sources report the capture of some Canadians near the City Hall. However, these were isolated forays, without cohesion, the efforts of gallant men determined to bring the fight to the elusive enemy, and could not affect the situation in any way.

Around seven o'clock, the guns of the West Headland, which in spite of continuous bombardment from the sea and air had never ceased to harass the men on the beach, suddenly switched their fire seawards, where a number of ships had been observed approaching. These were the twenty-six landing-craft carrying the Fusiliers Mont Royal – the floating reserve, who had been ordered in to reinforce Red Beach with the intention of launching an attack on the East Headland. But ill-luck, which had so dogged this expedition, played its part once more. A strong current, caused by the ebbing tide, swept the flotilla to the west, and with the beach obscured by smoke, many of the craft had no idea of their position until it was too late to turn away. As a result, much of the battalion was landed strung out along White Beach, half a mile from its proper position, and what was worse, nearly half of the unit were put ashore on a narrow strip of shingle to the west of the headland, off the main beach altogether. Here, faced with unscalable cliffs, they were trapped. To the east, towards White Beach, there is a concrete wall with pillboxes, impossible to assault on the narrow front available. To the west, machine-gun fire and grenades thrown from the cliffs overhead bar the outlet towards Pourville. There is no way out except by sea. Here on the narrow beach, nearly 300 of the Mont Royals, many of them wounded, must remain until the end of the day, unable to take part in the fight, helpless and frustrated.

Those of their comrades who landed on White Beach were met with an intense fire from the headland and from the houses behind the beach. Once again, all is confusion. Officers and men fall dead and wounded, some seek what shelter they can find behind the folds of the shingle and return the enemy fire. Others press grimly on through the storm and somehow reach the sea wall to join with the R.H.L.I. in clearing the upper part of the Casino. After fierce room-to-room fighting the building is captured and a way into the town opened. Covered by fire from the former German strong-point, some small groups of the R.H.L.I. and Mont Royals dash across the open and make their way through the narrow streets, attacking machine-gun posts at intersections, shooting down snipers from roof-tops and for a short while actually clearing the streets adjacent to the front. One body of Canadians attack the German positions in the hotels lining the Boulevard de Verdun. Coming in from the rear, they found many of the buildings on fire and deserted, but some were still in action and these they soon silenced. Not all Canadians at Dieppe were frustrated; some at least showed what they could do; but it could not last – strong enemy patrols were coming in from all directions. Some of the little groups found themselves cut off and were either killed or captured. Not many of them got back to the beach. One small party of the Mont Royals, led by Sergeant Dubuc, entered the town via the Rue de Sygogne, opposite the Casino, and turning east, proceeded towards the docks, probably by the Rue de la Barre and the Grande Rue. Sergeant Dubuc had travelled 3,000 miles and waited two and a half years for an opportunity to get to grips with the invaders of his motherland. Sitting about on the beach being shot at was not in his programme. When he came ashore and summed up the situation, he soon spotted an abandoned tank near by, and with one man from his platoon entered the tank and spent an enjoyable thirty minutes shooting up enemy positions on the West Hill. When there were no more shells left, he collected his party and set off through the town. Reaching the docks, the party killed some Germans on two barges, and then swinging right made their way along the railway line for about half a mile until they ran into a strong force of Germans. In the resulting gun battle the Canadians used up all their ammunition and were captured. The Germans forced them to remove their tunics and trousers, and left them standing in their underwear and boots in charge of a single guard. However, a little thing like the loss of his rifle and trousers did not deter Sergeant Dubuc. Enticing the sentry near to him by a ruse, he set upon him and with the aid of his comrades killed him. The party, clad in vests, pants and boots, then rushed off towards the beach, much to the astonishment of sundry French people encountered en route. Some of the men lost their way in the maze of narrow streets and were again captured, but some, including Sergeant Dubuc, succeeded in regaining the beach, where they found the evacuation in progress. Sergeant Dubuc spent the next hour carrying wounded men to the boats, among them being his Commanding Officer, Lt.-Col. Menard, who had been badly wounded at the moment of landing. For his gallantry and leadership Sergeant Dubuc was awarded the Military Medal.

There were many other acts of individual bravery which shone like bright threads in the drab picture of disaster that loomed over the Dieppe beaches, where conditions were steadily deteriorating as more and more enemy guns zeroed in on the foreshore. Under the wall and in the Casino the Canadians fought back savagely at their invisible enemy. Beside them and behind them on the stones lay their dead and wounded, and here and there, moving about amid the hail of bullets and mortar shells, were men of the Royal Canadian Army Medical Corps, carrying the injured to aid posts set up in the shelter of derelict tanks. Outstanding among the mercy workers on that dreadful morning was the chaplain of the R.H.L.I., Honorary Captain J. W. Foote. Ignoring the bullets and shells, he worked ceaselessly carrying wounded men to the aid posts, and at the withdrawal, after bearing many injured men to the boats, refused to be evacuated, preferring to remain with his men. After the war, he was decorated with the first Victoria Cross ever to be awarded to a Canadian chaplain.

Dieppe

A low-level photograph showing (top centre) a German soldier guarding the bridge over the Pollet channel at the entrance to the Inner Harbour. Note (top left) four workmen running for cover, while on the right two women stroll unconcernedly across the road

Some of No 4 Commandos landing at Vasterival

Landing-craft approaching the beach

Derelict tank in the Gardens opposite the gutted Grand Hotel. Red Beach

Lord Lovat and some of his Commandos after Dieppe

After the battle. Canadian wounded being tended by their comrades

Battle-weary
Commandos
disembarking
at Newhaven

Aftermath, White Beach

Meanwhile, on Red Beach at a point slightly to the east of the Tobacco Factory, brigadier Southam, commanding the 6th Brigade, had set up his Brigade H.Q. in a hole scooped out of the stones. His H.Q. party, and that of Brigadier Lett, commanding the 4th Brigade, had been distributed in four groups between different tank landing-craft, and of two H.Q. parties, Brigadier Southam was the only officer to get ashore. Brigadier Lett's craft had failed to land her tanks at the first attempt, and coming in again had been heavily shelled, all her crew killed and Brigadier Lett seriously wounded. Before becoming unconscious, he managed to delegate command of the 4th Brigade to Lt. Col. Labatt of the R.H.L.I., who had his Battalion H.Q. on the beach near the Casino.

Now Brigadier Southam, from his precarious position, tried to appraise the appalling situation which confronted him. It was only too clear that the first swift onslaught through the wire and into the enemy positions had failed under the murderous fire sweeping the beach. Everywhere the troops were pinned down; there was nothing for it but to dig in and wait.

The thunder of gunfire from seawards and the sight of the west hill shrouded in the smoke of bursting shells and bombs was encouraging but as time went on it became apparent that, far from the enemy fire diminishing under the naval and aerial bombardment, it was steadily increasing. The capture of the Casino at 7.12 a.m. offered a ray of hope, but the disaster to the Mont Royals dissipated any chance of exploiting this minor success.

Once the Casino was secured, Col. Labatt moved his skeleton Brigade-cum-Battalion H.Q. there, to find that some small parties had entered the town. Those who returned reported large concentrations of enemy troops sheltering behind the concrete street barriers and just waiting their opportunity to rush the beach.

As the long morning wore on, it was borne in on Col. Labatt that he and the men with him in the Casino were being cast for the role of rear-guard. Enemy pressure was steadily increasing; the houses on the Boulevard de Verdun, earlier cleared of Germans, had now been reoccupied and machine-guns were firing from them. The Canadian tanks, which had been prowling up and down the Gardens seeking a way into the town, had either been knocked out or withdrawn to the beach, where, buttoned up, they were doggedly fighting, shelling the West Hill and the houses behind the beach. But all the time, the German fire grew heavier; behind the barriers the enemy crouched, waiting to pounce. So long as the Casino held out he would not dare to do so, but once the fire from the Casino slackened, then a flood of German soldiers would surge out across the Gardens to mop up the beach. Away on the east end of the beach, some Germans had already infiltrated on to the foreshore and were enfilading the Essex Scottish from the shelter of the groynes. A message passed to the H.Q. ship via the Casino brought a destroyer in like an avenging angel to shell the enemy positions from close range, indeed, so close that as she turned away her stern struck bottom.

At ten o'clock Brigadier Southam received the signal to prepare to evacuate both beaches, starting at eleven o'clock. Orders to this effect were issued and some troops sent back to wait on the beach. Checking the defences of the Casino, it was found that ammunition was running low. At the present rate of firing it might last until one o'clock, and there was no hope of further supplies. Earlier, a landing-craft full of munitions had blown up on the beach near the Casino. Not that it mattered a lot; there was no one to unload it, anyway.

In the trenches behind the Casino, in the battered building and under the sea wall, the troops settled down for their last fight. Some would go, some would stay, nobody could tell what the next hour held for him.

On board H.M.S. *Calpe* the force commander and his staff were struggling to fit together a very incomplete picture of events ashore. By 7.30 a.m. it was known that Commando Group No. 4 had accomplished their set task at Varengeville and were safely re-embarked. The two leaders of the Yellow Beach flotilla had arrived with their news of the disaster to No. 3 Commando, and from Pourville had come reassuring news. But from Blue Beach at Puys there was no word. The flotilla leader, Lieut.-Commander Goulding, had reported in person at seven o'clock that he had successfully landed the regiment but was unaware that anything was amiss on the beach. What was happening at Puys?

The position on the main beach at Dieppe was equally obscure. Since the second wave of tanks had reported that they were about to land, no news whatsoever had come as to progress. The weight of enemy fire was increasing and it was becoming more and more difficult to approach the beach.

Somewhere about 6.40 a.m. a message purporting to come from Red Beach reported that the Essex Scottish were off the beach and advancing into the town. This was completely incorrect, and it appears that the actual signal sent was one from the '18' set with the Essex Scottish to Brigadier Southam, advising him that some men from Red Beach had crossed the Gardens and entered the houses opposite. The message was intercepted by *Calpe* and by the time it reached the force commander was grossly distorted. It was the first clear news of events on the centre beaches, and caused General Roberts to order in the Fusiliers Mont Royal to reinforce Red Beach and help in the attack on the East Hill. There was still a chance that the Royal Regiment were fighting their way on to this position from the rear, as planned, and it was now more than ever important that the powerful armament of the hill should be silenced.

At seven o'clock the Mont Royals set out for the beach, and shortly afterwards the first news from Blue Beach came to hand in the shape of a message asking to be taken off. As mentioned earlier, some landing-craft were dispatched to Puys on what was to prove a hopeless mission. At 7.12 a.m. came the news that the Casino had fallen, and this was followed at eight o'clock by another signal reporting that White Beach was under control. This message was false and almost certainly came from enemy sources, but it was accepted by the force commander, who decided that the time was ripe to exploit the situation on this beach. He had just learnt of the failure of the Mont Royals' landing, which meant that any attempt on the harbour was now impossible. The Royal Marine Commando were therefore in hand, and they were at once ordered to trans-ship into assault craft and move in to White Beach with the intention of circling through the town to attack the East Hill from the south.

Earlier H.M.S. *Locust* had made several gallant attempts to force the harbour entrance and land the Marine Commando, but each time had been driven off by intense and accurate shell fire, sustaining damage and casualties. Now the Marines trans-shipped into two T.L.C.s, with their C.O. Lt.-Col. J. Picton-Phillips, and at 8.30. a.m. in company with the seven French Chasseurs and several motor boats to give supporting fire, set off on the run-in. As the little flotilla emerged from the smoke screen and surged forward to the beach, a fiendish barrage of high explosives and machine-gun bullets tore into them, of a violence unsurpassed on that morning of violence. Lt.-Col. Picton-Phillips, in the leading T.L.C., at once realized the utter impossibility of landing his force in the face of such an appalling concentration of fire. Springing to the highest and most exposed part of his ship, he signalled with his arms to the following vessels to turn away, and as he fell to the deck, mortally wounded, died with the satisfaction of knowing he had saved his comrades.

Meanwhile the T.L.C., her naval crew dead, drove on to a sandbank some distance from the shore, stuck fast, and became a sitting target for the enemy guns. Any question in the minds of the surviving Marines as to what to do was quickly settled when fuel from leaking tanks seeping along the deck suddenly exploded into flame. Some essayed the short swim to the shore and made it. Others, not so lucky reddened the waters with their life's blood. Still others decided to swim out to sea hoping to be picked up. The bobbing heads became targets for the enemy and one by one disappeared. One 18-year-old Marine swam away from the beach, with bullets lashing the water around him but miraculously leaving him untouched. He had been alloted the task of hanging a Union Jack from the tower in the Dieppe Fish Market, but now was in danger of drowning from sheer exhaustion. His 'Mae West' had become partially undone and his heavy boots, which he was unable to unlace, tended to drag him down.

What follows he makes no attempt to explain, but some weeks previously he had learnt that his best friend, a bomber pilot, had been killed over Germany, and now, on the point of giving up the struggle, he became acutely conscious of his friends presence and heard his voice calling 'hold on, hold on'. Thus encouraged, the young Marine floated on his back for some time until picked up by a Flak ship and returned safely to England.

Evacuation

THE failure of the Royal Marine Commando to effect a landing brought to a close the offensive phase of the operation. There were still some thirty tanks in hand, but to commit them to the beaches in face of the ever-growing enemy fire would be madness. Soon after nine o'clock they were ordered to return home. The force commander and his staff now got down to the job of organizing the evacuation, which must commence at the earliest possible moment. Air-attacks were now being made on the ships, and the shelling from the shore was noticeably heavier. All heavy equipment brought ashore would have to be abandoned, and indeed there were grave doubts whether it would be possible to save any of the surviving troops. However, an attempt must and would be made, nobody had any doubts about that, so plans were formulated and orders issued. It would be at least two hours before the operation could commence. The R.A.F. needed time to prepare for a massive onslaught with smoke and H.E. bombs on the German positions. The attack would begin at eleven o'clock precisely and continue for half an hour, supported by every available gun in the remaining destroyers and motor boats. There would of necessity be a reduction in the fighter cover for some time, while aircraft refuelled and prepared for the final struggle, but this could not be helped.

Fortunately there was no shortage of landing-craft, in spite of losses, and the shocking casualties ashore would tend to make the operation speedier. The landing-craft were divided up, some to Pourville, some to Dieppe and a few to Puys for one last attempt. Earlier, one lone vessel had come from Puys with the few survivors of the Royal Regiment, and it was thought that men still lived on that beach.

The Luftwaffe, for the moment free of the attentions of

the R.A.F., stepped up their attacks on the fleet and on the beaches, where the troops were preparing to embark. The anti-aircraft guns on the warships were firing incessantly at the diving Stukas and had already scored several successes, while the artillery fire from the shore wakened to a new pitch of fury. It seemed the enemy had scented something – either another landing or a withdrawal – and was determined to prevent it. The heavy smoke-screens being laid out at sea alarmed him, and a terrific barrage covered the water up to some hundreds of yards off shore.

Exactly at eleven o'clock, the R.A.F. swept in and blotted out Dieppe beach and the headlands behind dense fog, and dead on time the first of the landing-craft appeared at the water's edge, dimly seen in the swirling clouds of smoke. Thankfully, men rose from their cramped positions under the wall and from the hollows and folds in the shingle, and slowly moved out over that tortured beach, now almost 200 yards wider, as the tide ebbed. Ghostlike in the grey mist, they made their way towards the sea, supporting each other, carrying those who could not walk, heading to the promise of safety. For the space of a minute there was a pause in the enemy firing, as gunners groped for targets in the enveloping fog, and then the whole of that mile-long expanse of shingle and sand erupted into flame and smoke as the German guns fired blindly into the greyness. All the heavy field-guns and mortars sited round the town and in the streets, all the armament of the remaining anti-aircraft and anti-tank guns, all machine-guns and rifles poured a colossal weight of fire on the beach and the verges of the sea. Landing-craft reeled and shuddered and sank beneath the blind blows of the fury unleashed upon them. The drifting wraiths of mist were split and torn apart by exploding shells and laced by the fiery threads of tracer. Men died and drowned in the shallow water, as they reached out their hands to the ships. Others, hauled into the fancied safety of a vessel, found themselves flung back into the sea as their spurious refuge was blasted apart by heavy shells. Some, wiser perhaps than their fellows, once more sought the shelter of the walls, and watched with anguished eyes as Death strode the beach, his finger flickering aimlessly amongst the orderly lines of men, touching first this one and then that.

For more than an hour the barrage crashed down on the

beach and the little ships came in on their errands of rescue, until more than 300 men were lifted from the grip of the enemy. But now the smoke was clearing, and the landing-craft were clear targets as they sought once more to approach the wide strip of sand. Many men still lived on that dreadful place of death, and somehow they must be given the opportunity to escape. A signal was sent to the men in the Casino, telling them to prepare to make a dash for the beach the instant the landing-craft appeared. To them, above all, was due whatever success had so far been attained in the rescue operation. They had defeated all enemy attempts to break through to the beach, and now it was time to go. As the landing-craft broke through the smoke-screen and swept in to the shore over the last few hundred yards of clear water, they were buffeted and battered by a tremendous barrage. Great gouts of water rose up on all sides, and ahead a wall of flame and smoke from exploding shells and mortar bombs cut them off from the sea wall. Desperately the ships fought to get in, twisting and turning, often flung off course by the blast of a near miss. Here and there on the beach a little figure would rise from the stones and run to the water's edge, only to vanish in an uprush of searing flame and black smoke. Close inshore, disdaining the cover of the smoke-screens, destroyers and motor boats were blasting away at the shore, their sirens screaming the recall. But it was hopeless. The rescue boats could not get in and the men on the beach could not penetrate the steel curtain between them and safety.

At 12.30 a signal was sent to the beachmaster ashore saying, 'If no more evacuation possible, withdraw.' The message, as received by him, read, 'No more evacuation possible, withdraw.' As he had already arrived at the same decision, no harm was done, and under the frightful conditions on the beach at the time the error is understandable. Accordingly the evacuation was terminated, and although the Navy begged to be allowed to try once more, the request was turned down and the fleet drew off to take station for the return journey.

Having seen the convoy under way, H.M.S. *Calpe* returned for one last look at the battlefield. At full speed and under heavy fire, she steamed along close to the beach, but there was nothing to be seen – only the pitiable evidence of defeat, derelict tanks, stranded and burning ships, and everywhere on the torn and shattered shore khaki-clad bodies. The flower of Canada lay there on the blood-splashed stones, crumpled and dead. Beyond the West Hill, under the high cliffs, the unlucky Mont Royals were seen crowded on the narrow beach. As the destroyer tore past, her guns blazing at the hill, men waved and some shook their fists as they saw the vessel turn away. They were the forgotten men — landed in the wrong place, out of the fight from the start and now abandoned. Is it any wonder they were bitter?

As *Calpe* pulled away into the fog, a message came from Brigadier Southam. Since establishing his makeshift H.Q. in the shingle near the junction of Red and White Beaches, Southam had kept in intermittent contact with the H.Q. ship by means of a radio set in a scout car. For part of the day he also had been in touch with the Essex Scottish on his left through an '18' set working on Red Beach, but had no contact, except by runner, with the R.H.L.I.

His was a most unhappy position, a Brigadier without a command, bereft of his H.Q. staff and proper communications, cut off from all contact with his own brigade, the 6th, the majority of which had landed at Pourville, and quite unable to exert any influence over the course of events at Dieppe.

Now, at 13.08 hours, his last signal had come in.

'There seems to be a mass surrender of our troops on the beach. Our people in the Casino have also surrendered.'

However, this was not quite correct. Not all the troops surrendered at this time. Somewhere about the centre of the beach, Lt.-Col. Labatt came wading ashore for his second landing, when the vessel in which he was being evacuated sank from a direct hit.

Here he found upwards of 200 men, sheltering behind the many wrecked vehicles, the majority of them wounded and in a desperate condition. Many of the wounded were lying in the water and in danger of drowning. Col. Labatt set the unwounded men to work removing their comrades to a safer position, and then, encouraged by the naval Beachmaster's statement that more landing-craft were coming in for a further attempt at evacuation, he organized a defensive position and continued to fight. After some time the troops to the east and west were observed going up through the wire on to the promenade, and Labatt realized that his was the only group left on the beach. However using immobilized tanks and landing-craft as cover they kept going until a message from the beachmaster informed them that the evacuation had been terminated. By this time the rapidly rising tide had driven men out from cover on to the open beach, and deciding that further resistance was futile, Labatt sent a German prisoner off to announce that they were prepared to surrender. German troops quickly appeared on the sea wall; the Canadians stood up (those who could stand) with arms upraised, and it was all over. This did not prevent some trigger-happy Germans from throwing a few grenades among the helpless wounded lying on the beach.

For some reason not explained, practically all the rescue attempts at Dieppe was concentrated on White Beach. Apparently the unhappy plight of the Mont Royals was not appreciated aboard the H.Q. ship, and no landing-craft were sent in for them. The Essex Scottish on Red Beach were also ignored, although it is reported that some vessels intended for this beach went instead to Pourville. Another report suggests that a flotilla of craft on the way in were attacked by German aircraft and all but one of the ships sunk. There is no doubt that the Luftwaffe succeeded in greatly disorganizing the rescue work, repeated machine-gun attacks scattering the ships and forcing them back to the cover of the war vessels and anti-aircraft guns. These attacks, in conjunction with the colossal shelling of the beach and sea approaches, brought about an early end to the evacuation.

Official returns show that some 370 men were taken off Dieppe beach, while left behind were nearly 500 dead and over 1,100 prisoners, many of them wounded. The Essex Scottish and the Mont Royals suffered particularly heavy losses in prisoners.

Apart from the incident related above, the British wounded were well treated. For them and for their unwounded comrades the war was over. They had had their brief hour of glory – that hour they had looked forward to through many boring and arduous months. They had had their baptism of fire, and what a bitter and frustrating experience it had been.

As the fleet sailed towards England, they were constantly harassed by bomber and fighter attacks. The Luftwaffe were out in force, using squadrons from as far away as Germany in a desperate effort to destroy the invaders. Terrific air combats developed, many of them far away from the Dieppe area, as the R.A.F. broke up the large German formations long before they could reach the target area. Individual planes got through to machine-gun and bomb the ships, and unfortunate last-minute casualties were sustained. One destroyer was hit by a jettisoned bomb and sank, but generally the Luftwaffe pilots were so harried by the Spitfires that they were unable to concentrate on their deadly work. By late afternoon the flotilla had arrived off their home ports, only to find that arrangements for the handling of the numerous wounded had gone awry. Four tank landing-craft had been equipped as hospital ships, but as it proved impossible to get them to the beaches they had been sent home early in the action. As a result the wounded men had to be accommodated on the destroyers and motor boats, which were filled to overflowing. Disembarkation of stretcher cases from the narrow and crowded decks was a major problem, and much delay and unnecessary suffering resulted. Just another unhappy muddle in a day notable for unhappy muddles.

Navigation

In the foregoing chapters the part played by the Royal Navy has hardly been mentioned, beyond the bald statement that the Navy carried the troops to the beaches and took them off again.

My story in the main set out to deal with the land battle and events ashore, and it would require another book to describe adequately the exploits of the Navy during the action.

Suffice it to say that the Navy performed a prodigious task in bringing a large number of assorted vessels, some slow, some fast, across seventy miles of sea, through minefields, in total darkness and radio silence, without a mishap.

Once arrived at the dispersal point, many of the 6,000 troops had then to be trans-shipped into smaller craft and delivered ashore at eight different points on the enemy-held coast, all within a fifteen-minute time-limit. An operation of the utmost complexity, calling for a high degree of professional competence and skill, and, as it turned out, of sublime courage.

Of courage there was no lack, but that last fine degree of professional skill was not in evidence on a few occasions. Unfortunate errors were made, which brought about unfortunate results; these probably could not be avoided under the circumstances, and must not be allowed to detract from the momentous feat of organization and timing carried out by the Navy.

As we have seen, six of the eight landings went in on time, those at Berneval and Puys being late. The tragic aspect of the disaster to the Berneval contingent is that it need not have happened. The German convoy had been detected by British shore-based radar almost from the time it left Boulogne, and when it was realized that the two flotillas were on a collision course, a warning signal was flashed at 1.27 a.m. to the two screening destroyers *Brocklesby* and *Slazak*, and a further warning sent at 2.44 a.m. Neither of these messages was received by the protecting force, nor were they picked up by *Calpe*, but some of the other craft in the main fleet logged them. Indeed, even had the force commander in *Calpe* received the messages, it is difficult to see what he could have done about them without breaking wireless silence.

Slazak was a Polish destroyer and her Polish commander the senior officer of the two ships. It has been suggested that this fact contributed to the failure to intercept the German vessels, but in what way is not clear. Undoubtedly there was an error of judgment in assuming the firing came from the shore, but once the battle opened the damage was done so far as No. 3 Commando was concerned. By the time the destroyers could reach the scene the landing-craft would have scattered, and the most they could hope to do was to engage the enemy vessels. The escorts' task was to fend off any enemy craft, and as luck would have it they were on another course when the hostile craft approached. The great misfortune here was in the non-receipt of the two signals.

It seems strange that Portsmouth did not send a special signal to Commander Wyburd on the steam gunboat leading the Berneval flotilla, giving him the position, speed and course of the enemy ships and so enabling him to take avoiding action. But nothing further was done, and back in Portsmouth a young member of the W.R.N.S., with a brother in No. 3 Commando, watched on a radar screen the two plots steadily and inexorably approaching each other, watched until, at 3.47 a.m. precisely, they mingled.

The Puys landings were delayed by an incident at the trans-shipment point which should not have occurred, but was always likely in the confusion of loading dozens of assault craft in the open sea, in total darkness, forming them into their correct columns and picking up their guide ships.

Both these mishaps were to have fatal consequences, for the men involved and for the expedition as a whole, and the planners had endeavoured to provide against such happenings by allowing wireless silence to be broken if, in the opinion of the senior officers, the success of any landing was jeopardized by delay or casualties. As we have seen, Commander Wyburd was unable to report owing to the destruction of his wireless, and the Royal Regiment heading for Puys apparently did not report their late arrival on the beach.

The Pourville landings suffered from faulty navigation, when the Navy put the South Sasks ashore on the west or right bank of the River Scie, instead of landing them *astride* the river, and then unloaded the Cameron Highlanders astride the river, when, in fact, they should have been landed complete on the west bank. That the Camerons were half an hour late was perhaps not so important. This was due in part to the wish of the Commanding Officer, Lt.-Col. Gostling, who wanted to land ten minutes after the pre-arranged time, to give the South Sasks more time to clear the beach. As it was, errors of speed and course prolonged the delay to thirty minutes.

At Dieppe navigational errors resulted in the first wave of tanks being fifteen minutes late, thus delaying the assault force the support so desperately needed at the moment of landing. The tanks were to engage the pillboxes covering the beach, but in view of the number of unsuspected anti-tank guns firing on them it is open to question whether the situation would have been in any way improved by a prompt arrival.

It is only fair to the Navy to mention that the standard of training of the landing-craft crews at this time was far from perfect, and under the circumstances they performed a magnificent job. Getting the troops ashore was only the beginning of the Navy's work. From then on, they had to stand off the coast within range of the enemy guns, give artillery support to the assault groups, make trip after trip to the beaches to pick up wounded, and at the last, evacuate the survivors, all the time under a fire of undreamt-of ferocity.

It had been thought to be impossible for the fleet to stand in close to the beach unless the coastal-defence batteries were silenced, but with all but one of them in action all the time, supported by the entirely unexpected guns in the East Headland, the Navy were confronted with an additional problem. However, they carried on with their tasks, using smoke-cover whenever possible, ever in danger from the constantly growing number of air-attacks and the never-ending shelling.

The destroyers and motor boats kept up a steady barrage on the enemy positions, often approaching close inshore in full view of the German gunners, and rising to superhuman pitch during the evacuation. The destroyer H.M.S. *Albrighton*, during the early stages of the battle, put up a display of fancy gunnery when shelling the tobacco factory. Controlled by her forward observation officer, who was ashore on Red Beach, *Albrighton* started at the top left-hand window and planted her shells through each window in turn, right across the floor, then dropping to the next storey came back from right to left, and so on down to the ground floor.

All through the day the landing-craft plied to and from the beaches, scorning the enemy's fire and suffering heavy casualties among their crews, but there were always men ready to replace those killed or wounded, and never once did the unprotected vessels fail to answer a call from the shore. At the end the naval crews reached new heights of valour in their efforts to bring off the troops. Braving a colossal barrage that tore the water to shreds up to 500 yards out to sea, they forced their little ships through to the beach, protected by nothing but the smoke-screen that hid them from German eyes but gave no cover from German shells and bullets. When all hope of further evacuation was abandoned, they offered to make one more attempt to penetrate the curtain of steel that cut them off from the shore, but were not permitted to do so.

When at last the fleet turned for home, many of the warships were down to their last few shells, but no German surface craft attempted to interfere with the convoy. The Luftwaffe did, however, and the anti-aircraft gunners had no respite from attacks by individual aircraft.

Mistakes there may have been, but the day could be chalked up as a victory for the Royal Navy, who did all they were asked to do and far more than anyone had anticipated.

Protection

ONE of the outstanding features of Operation 'Jubilee' was the high degree of protection afforded to the fleet and the troops on shore by the R.A.F. At his headquarters at No. 11 Group Fighter Command, Air Marshal Leigh-Mallory had at his disposal fifty-six squadrons of fighters and eleven squadrons of light bombers and Recce Mustangs. With this force it was hoped to deal the Luftwaffe a series of smashing blows whenever and wherever they appeared. It was a long-awaited opportunity, welcomed with delight by the R.A.F. The air liaison officer on board H.M.S. *Calpe* was Air Commodore Cole, who sustained severe wounds from a machine-gun attack by a German fighter at the very end of the battle, when the ships were proceeding homewards.

The ball was opened at 4.45 a.m. by the Spitfires' attack on the lighthouse at Pointe D'Ailly, and was followed up by cannon-firing Spitfires, Hurricane fighter-bombers and Bostons blasting the Dieppe sea front, while Blenheims bombed the two headlands and laid smoke over the East Hill. Other squadrons attacked the German batteries behind Dieppe and on the flanks – attacks which were pressed home in face of intense anti-aircraft fire, but which never succeeded in silencing the guns.

Up to nine o'clock the R.A.F. had the sky to themselves, very few German aircraft appearing, but from that time on they came in ever-increasing numbers, swerving and spir-alling out of the clouds to attack the low-flying bombers as they harassed the German batteries. Now the battle was joined in earnest and aerial combats developed high above the smoke-shrouded battlefield below.

The tardy reaction of the Luftwaffe was strange – it may have been that so many pilots were absent from their airfields, or they may have been deliberately held back until more was known of the British intentions. However, once they started to move they came from all parts, Germany, Holland and Belgium, and by eleven o'clock the R.A.F. were strained to the limit. Great formations of German bombers were approaching high in the sky, but always the never-failing radar on the English coast spotted them and down from above came the dreaded Spitfires, machine-guns and cannons flaming, to scatter the black-crossed planes, forcing them to jettison their bombs and seek the shelter of the ground. Time after time, protected by squadrons of F.W. 190s, the enemy bombers tried to get through to the fleet, but always the Spitfires were there to drive them off.

Single planes got through to attack the evacuating troops and the fleet, but no organized bombing formations came within miles of the target area.

Meanwhile, squadrons of Spitfires and Bostons kept up attacks against the German positions, constantly harassed by German fighters. It is reckoned by those who should know that the unremitting attacks on the two headlands and the inland batteries saved the near-disaster on the beaches from becoming complete. By the end of the day one-third of the entire German Air Force in the west was thought to have been destroyed or damaged, and the R.A.F. had won their greatest victory since the Battle of Britain. But more important than relative losses, they had kept their promise to protect the convoy. Ask any of the people of Dieppe for their outstanding memory of that noisy day, and they will answer, 'The roar of the R.A.F. planes skimming over our roof-tops in never-ending streams.' The official account states that almost 3,000 sorties were flown that day by the Royal Air Force.

Exultation

SOMEWHERE about 2 a.m. the moon set and it was very dark. In his post at the end of Dieppe Pier, the naval sentry scanned the dark sea through powerful night-glasses. This was the time when a man's eyes played tricks, and one was likely to see the outline of monstrous ships heading relentlessly for the coast. One had to be careful. It wouldn't do to awaken the *Unteroffizier* to look at a mirage. At three o'clock and not a moment before, he was to be called to switch on the light which would guide in the two convoys creeping along the coast under cover of the night. In the meantime there was nothing to do but strain one's eyes staring into the blackness and try to forget the minutes that dragged by on leaden feet. It was intensely still – only the faint suck and slap of the tide against the weed-covered stones broke the silence. Above his head loomed the camouflaged bulk of the lighthouse, which soon would send its subdued wink seawards to reassure the groping convoys. He looked at his watch: time to call the officer. Descending, he wakened the *Unteroffizier*, who at once went to the control room and switched on the mechanism which set the light flashing and revolving.

Climbing to the look-out platform, the *Unteroffizier* stood beside the sentry and stared out into the night. Above his head the light turned steadily, its thin ray piercing the darkness like a sword-blade. In another hour the two convoys should be off the harbour, flashing their identification signals, and then his job was over for the night. He remained on the platform for a long time peering seawards. Across that dark sea, on such a night as this, a great fleet might come carrying an invasion force. He hoped that if it ever happened he would not be stuck up here like a winkle on a pin. With a word to the sentry he turned to go below, when suddenly, away to the north-east, the darkness was split by jagged orange flashes, and the thunder of gun-fire came rolling over the water. Both men stared through their binoculars, but nothing could be seen except the intermittent flicker of the gun-blasts. The *Unteroffizier* went below to the telephone and reported the matter to the duty officer at Naval H.Q. The officer listened without comment and with a curt '*Danke*' hung up. Probably the west-bound convoy had run into some prowling enemy warship. For about twenty minutes the battle continued, gradually diminishing until all was quiet once more. His signals-crew were uneasy, gazing out to sea and talking in low voices. He growled at them and they fell silent. There was a strange tension in the air. He found himself listening hard, straining his ears for sounds from seaward.

He was acutely aware of danger: something was out there in the night, he could hear a faint grumble of sound that seemed to come up from the sea itself. Of course – what a fool he was! – the east-bound convoy must be almost in sight by now. He swept his glasses in a wide arc. Nothing to starboard – was that a ship to port? He nudged the sentry and pointed. Yes – a ship, two ships, three ships. Challenging signals flashed out and were answered, and in a few minutes the three vessels slid quietly past the pier-head into the harbour. It was 4.30 a.m.

As yet there was no sign of the other convoy, which would certainly have scattered when the enemy ships appeared. The two men stood with their glasses to their eyes searching the sea. Suddenly the sentry said, 'Look, sir, dead ahead – a ship.' Through the powerful night-glasses there appeared the dim outline of a ship, a long way out, moving eastwards – just a faint, dark shadow. 'Give her a signal,' the *Unteroffizier* ordered, and the lamp began to flash its question. Again and again the challenge went out without reply. The mystery ship, vague and unsubstantial in the gloom, continued on its course. The *Unteroffizier* rushed to the telephone and reported an unidentified vessel to Navy H.Q. The same bored voice replied with the same curt '*Danke*', but this time there were more results. In a few seconds a broad stream of light tore a path through the darkness and lit up the eastern sea like daylight, revealing clearly a small warship with a long line of motor boats strung out behind it.

The *Unteroffizier* swore. 'Those are British ships,' he said, running once again to the telephone. As he returned to the look-out platform, he became aware of the distant hum of aircraft engines, and suddenly the sky to the west was illuminated by flares and the flashes of bursting shells.

'That's over Quiberville,' the sentry said. 'Wonder what they're after there.'

Even as he spoke, the noise of gun-fire swelled ominously and the hum of aircraft grew to a roar as a flight passed directly overhead, drawing fire from the guns on the East Headland, which opened up in a sudden shattering blast of sound.

The *Unteroffizier* looked at his watch: a quarter to five. Dawn was at hand – he could just make out the outline of the anti-tank gun mounted on the pier, a hundred yards away. The Dieppe guns fell silent, but inland and from the west came an uneasy muttering and the thud of heavy guns. Now suddenly beyond the West Headland flares rose into the sky, and distinctly on the faint breeze came the hammering of machine-guns and the boom of artillery.

'That sounds like Pourville,' the sentry said. 'Do you think it's the invasion?'

The *Unteroffizier* snapped at him, 'How the hell should I know?' He was nervous – he didn't like this at all. Pacing back and forth on the narrow platform, he heard the anti-tank gun's crew running to their posts, and then a sudden burst of gun-fire from behind the East Headland lit the greying sky with staccato flashes. A shout from the sentry: 'There're ships out there – dozens of them.' He snatched up his glasses and focused them out to sea. Yes, by God, there are ships, grey shapes dimly seen in the gloom.

As he stared in sheer amazement, a line of jagged orange flame stabbed out along the dark horizon, followed by a stunning explosion of sound and the shrill scream of shells hurtling landwards. At once the dark gash of the sea front was transformed into a mad whirl of bursting high explosives, and then down from the sky came a swarm of aircraft with roaring motors and stuttering cannon blasting the Gardens and hotels. The little group at the pier-head huddle together in sheer fright, but the *Unteroffizier*, quickly pulling himself together, orders them to their positions.

'Get that machine-gun manned, this looks like it.'

Now red and orange tracer come in arcs out to sea, the sky above the town is filled with shell-bursts and flares. From the east and west cliffs and from the high ground inland spouts of flame lick upwards, as the A.A. batteries pound out their challenge to the low-flying planes. From their exposed position on the pier-head the signals-party can see the whole expanse of the beach, but seawards there is a monstrous bank of fog or smoke, drifting to the shore. Out of this, barely visible in the misty greyness, comes a host of small craft surging towards the land.

The *Unteroffizier* screams 'Fire!' and the machine-gun begins to stutter, sending its ribbons of tracer reaching out to the swiftly-moving vessels. The anti-tank gun near by opens fire, the crash of the explosions seeming to split their skulls apart. Then suddenly all that dark coast is lit with stabs and flickers of flame, as the beach-defence guns open up with a colossal roar of sound. At once all is confusion and noise. Up and down the beach and out over the water fiery threads of tracer weave a deadly pattern. Great bursts of red flame and gusts of black smoke erupt along the verge of the sea. The *Unteroffizier* keeps his machine-gun firing, although now the smoke-cloud obscures the beach and the sea. All around them is dirty white fog, reducing visibility to a couple of hundred yards. Now and again the vague shape of a vessel appears only to vanish in the all-pervading greyness.

Suddenly out of the fog, heading for the pier, a low, grey motor boat appears, white foam at her prow, her forward guns spitting fire. Instantly a hail of small shells smashes into the gun position and against the tower behind. Smoke and flying steel fill the enclosure, the machine-gun is blasted from its mounting, the gunners slump to the ground dead, and the *Unteroffizier*, his throat torn open by red-hot splinters, falls across their bodies. A cloud of white dust from the shattered stonework overhead settles slowly over the bloody corpses.

The motor boat, swinging to starboard, turns the full force of her broadside on the anti-tank gun. From fifty yards' range the concentrated fire engulfs the gun and her crew. In a sheet of flame the gun explodes and the motor boat, her work done, turns away into the fog.

At German Divisional Headquarters at Envermu the

night of 18–19th August had been quiet, enlivened only by a report of an attack on a convoy somewhere off Berneval. The duty officer yawned as he looked at his watch: 4.45 a.m. Soon it would be daylight and his relief would appear. He pushed aside the paper-work on his desk, and as he did so the telephone rang and an excited voice reported what seemed to be an attack on the beach defences at Ste Marguérite, near Quiberville. The forward posts were in action, but nothing was known about the enemy strength.

The duty officer immediately sent an orderly to awaken the chief of Staff, and telephoned a message to the 15-cm battery behind Varengeville, warning them of a possible attack. Further signals were now coming in reporting aerial activity over the whole divisional area, and indeed the sound of distant ack-ack fire could be heard from the direction of the coast.

When the Chief of Staff, General Hoffmann, arrived, he glanced through the sheaf of messages on his desk and said, 'Call the General Oberst and get more news from Quiberville.' Just then an orderly brought a signal from Dieppe reporting some twenty landing-craft sailing along the coast in an easterly direction. General Hoffmann studied the map before him, pondering, then snapped, 'Send out the general alarm.' It was three minutes to five o'clock.

The divisional commander, General Haase, arrived shortly, looking astonished. 'I can hardly believe it,' he said. 'It must be a Commando raid. Thank God I didn't cancel the alert last night.' An officer came up and reported loss of contact by telephone with Varengeville. They were being called up by radio but had not answered. A few minutes later came a message from Pourville: 'Large number of enemy landing on beach, position confused, report later.' This was followed at 5.10 by a signal from Puys: 'Strong force enemy craft about to land on beach.'

The general looked grim. 'By God, this is no Commando raid. This looks like invasion – who would have thought it? – at the last possible minute. What have we got at Puys?'

An officer replied, 'One platoon of the 571st and one platoon of the Luftwaffe.'

The General looked at the Chief of Staff. 'Not a lot, but it's a difficult beach to get off. What about artillery?'

'There's a field-battery behind the village and some Pak

[anti-tank guns] covering the beach,' the Chief of Staff answered.

General Haase walked to the window and threw it open, gazing open into the dawn sky. Towards the coast the flicker of reflected gun-flashes could be seen in the sky, and borne on the faint westerly breeze came the muted thunder of the guns.

An officer came and reported: 'Dieppe signals heavy air-attacks on water front and West Hill positions. Pourville reports enemy troops in the village.'

The Chief of Staff said, 'Looks like a big show, sir.'

The General nodded. 'The next half-hour should tell us a lot.'

Just then the telephone tinkled on the general's desk. The Chief of Staff picked up the receiver and spoke, then suddenly jerking erect, his eyes seeking the general's face, he repeated the message coming over the wire: 'Large force of enemy troops landing on Dieppe beach under cover of smoke and bombardment from sea and air. Being heavily engaged by all units.'

The general was smiling grimly. 'Tell them to report every five minutes.' He glanced at his watch: 5.25 a.m. 'Alert all units.' For the next fifteen minutes everybody was busy, all engaged in the complex business of getting the division on the move.

Alone at his desk, the general sat staring at a large-scale map of the district. A report had come in of an attack on Berneval, which meant that a front of some eleven miles was being assaulted – from Varengeville on the left to Berneval on the right. Until he learnt how these various attacks were developing, he could do nothing – the divisional reserves were alerted and ready to move, but lack of transport was a problem. He would have to be very careful not to commit any units to the wrong sectors. At a quarter to six there was still no news of the enemy who had got inland on the left. The Varengeville battery reported all quiet and were awaiting the order to put down barrage fire on the Dieppe approaches. They had fired some salvoes at craft off Pourville, but it had been impossible to see the result. Until he knew what was out at sea the general could not give the order to fire. Ammunition was too scarce to waste on empty sea-space.

He called the Luftwaffe officer on his staff. 'When am I

going to get the Luftwaffe reports?' He spoke angrily and the officer flushed.

'Sir, we sent out three reconnaissance planes and none have either reported or returned. There are hundreds of Spitfires out there.'

The general snapped: 'Then send three more. I must know what the enemy has out at sea. Also find out what your people are doing about these hundreds of Spitfires.'

The Chief of Staff now approached, looking grave. 'They've taken Pourville and are advancing towards the radar station and Quatre Vents Farm. There has been a further landing at Pourville – most of the positions covering the beach have been knocked out.'

The general looked at his map. 'Send in the cyclist company from Cucures to attack Pourville from the south, and bring up the anti-tank company from Offranville towards Petit Appeville to cover Quatre Vents from the rear.'

An orderly appeared at his elbow. 'Signal from Varengeville, sir. The battery reports attack from the north.'

The general glanced at the Chief of Staff. 'How the hell did they get there through the minefields?' To the orderly: 'Keep in radio contact with the battery.'

Just then the Luftwaffe officer returned, looking worried. 'Sir, the Luftwaffe have not enough fighters available to make any impression on the large number of enemy aircraft. Most of the pilots are away on night leave and are not due back until eight o'clock. We have asked H.Q. for bombers, and some squadrons are coming from Holland and Germany, but will not arrive until at least eleven o'clock.'

The general fumed. 'It's always the same, never any co-operation, the Army are always left to fight it out as best they can.'

The arrival of an officer with a message averted the threatened storm. 'Sir, we have lost radio contact with Varengeville.'

The general pondered for a moment, then said, 'Send an officer on a motor cycle to reconnoitre the position and also get a strong patrol from Ouville to the battery position.'

By six o'clock the over-all situation appeared satisfactory – Dieppe was holding out well and reported that the enemy fire was too light and inaccurate to hamper the defenders seriously, but it was still impossible to see what was out at sea owing to the very thick smoke being used. So far only destroyers and small motor boats were engaged, but cannon-firing fighters and light bombers were keeping up steady attacks against all positions. From Puys the news was good – the attack had been held and so far none of the enemy had got off the beach. Berneval reported an assault by six landing-craft, and here too the enemy had failed to make any progress. Only on the left was there cause for anxiety – the enemy had an unknown number of men ashore on this flank and so far there was no news of their movements. The general was on the point of ordering a signal to be sent to Pourville, when he was handed a message reporting that a large body of enemy troops were pressing inland from the village, moving along the west bank of the Scie. He discussed this latest development with his staff and came to the conclusion that these troops, about a battalion, were heading for the airfield at St. Aubyn, or alternatively hoping to attack Dieppe from the rear.

Studying his map, the general ordered, 'Bring up the 1st Battalion from Ouville. Half will swing left-handed and go straight for Pourville, while the other half will head for Petit Appeville and link up with the Anti-Tank Company, which should be in position there shortly. We must hold them at the Scie bridge at Appeville and at the same time cut their line of retreat. They must not cross that bridge.'

A message was now received from Berneval reporting the battery under attack from a large number of the enemy, who had surrounded the position.

The general's jaw dropped. 'Berneval – but it can't be, no troops got off the beach there.' He glared at the Chief of Staff. 'I said those batteries should be put inside our perimeter defences – and now look what happens.'

Another message was handed to him. 'My God,' he said. 'Criel reports sighting ships off shore. What have we got there?'

The officers consulted for a moment. 'Two platoons of the 572nd Regiment.'

'Not enough,' barked the general. 'We'll have to send the divisional reserve from Eu, motorized.'

The transport officer spoke up. 'Sir, I'm afraid there are not enough lorries.'

'Then send them in cars, buses, anything that will run, take every vehicle you require.' The transport officer ran off, and turning to the Chief of Staff, the general ordered, 'If there is no attack on Criel, see that they turn down the Eu-Dieppe road towards Berneval. I want a patrol from Criel along the cliffs towards the battery position, and a strong patrol from Le Tréport moving along the cliffs to Criel. If the enemy gets ashore in this area he may try to cut the Eu-Dieppe road, and we must see that he doesn't.'

A signal from Dieppe now arrived, reporting that tanks had been landed, some of which had got on to the Promenade, but none had succeeded in breaking through the anti-tank barriers. The general looked thoughtful. 'He must mean business if he is using tanks,' he remarked.

The Chief of Staff consulted the map. 'We have the 302nd Anti-Tank Company moving into Dieppe – they should be there by eight o'clock.'

Another signal from Dieppe reported a second landing of tanks, but these also had been unsuccessful. The general was pleased, particularly as the message mentioned that all the assault troops had been pinned down under the sea wall and none had as yet entered the town. 'Our recruits here are not keeping their heads down,' he said with a smile.

An orderly brought in cups of coffee on a tray, and taking one the general walked to the open window. To his astonishment the landscape was veiled in thick grey fog. He called his officers over to look, and as they crowded round him one said, 'It's the enemy smoke-screen from Dieppe.'

'Nonsense,' said the general. 'How could it have travelled this far?'

'He's right, sir,' said the Chief of Staff. 'Dieppe reported an incredibly thick and clinging smoke-screen over our batteries in the East Hill, so much so that they couldn't fire until six o'clock. They are using it at sea also, and our gunners only get fleeting glimpses of the ships. It seems better than anything we have; why, you could land an army in daylight under cover of it.'

Leaving the window, the general went back to his desk. Reports and messages continued to pour in. So far things were going well, although he was worried about the left flank and by the absence of reports from aerial reconnaissance. He was puzzled about the position on the right, where the battery at Berneval were still being attacked, but there seemed to be no great danger here and reinforcements were on the move towards the area. Berneval must have been mistaken in saying that no enemy troops got off the beach. Some certainly had, but if not from Berneval, then from where? He looked at his map. What about Belleville?

He called to his Chief of Staff. 'What have we got at Belleville?'

'Nothing, sir,' was the reply. 'It's only a small beach and is very heavily wired at the only possible exit.' The Chief of Staff looked at the general. 'You're thinking the attack on the battery came from there?'

'Yes, I am, and I think we should send a patrol to find out. I don't want to take any men from either Puys or Berneval just yet. See if you can make contact with any patrols in the area. That battery hasn't fired a shot this morning – surely to God they can look after themselves, they must have upwards of two hundred men there. Look – send them a signal to mount a counter-attack immediately instead of just sitting there on their bottoms being shot at.'

The general sighed. What have they left me? Just a bunch of incompetent cowardly bastards and raw recruits, no transport, no aeroplanes, arguments over every request for more ammunition. Why the hell did he have to attack Russia, anyway? Listening to the distant rumble of gun-fire that had continued since dawn, he chuckled to himself. 'There goes their bloody ammunition – at this rate we will use it all by evening.'

His Chief of Staff came in with a message from Dieppe reporting a further enemy landing there, immediately beneath the West Hill, and some hundreds of men put ashore to the west of the hill on a narrow beach from which there was no way out.

The general grunted. 'What the hell did they do that for? Those cliffs are unscalable.' He studied his map once more. 'See that there are some M.G.s on the cliffs in case they try to break out towards Pourville.'

The little flag that indicted the enemy force in behind Pourville was being moved slowly forward. It now stood just short of Bernouville Wood. 'They're going for the airfield,' said an officer.

'Good,' said the general. 'The farther they go, the more

chance we have to cut them off. What's the latest from Pour-ville?'

An officer spoke up. 'Strong enemy attacks against Quatre Vents and rear of the West Hill being held. Some of our positions on the cliff top have been overrun, but heavy pressure is being maintained against the town.' A telephone tinkled. 'Commander, Dieppe, for you, General.'

The general listened, a little smile breaking over his face. He put back the receiver and said, 'We are picking up the enemy radio signals, some in code and some straight. Get me the radio officer.'

When the man appeared, the general explained the position, telling him, 'Send these signals to the enemy.' He scribbled on a pad: 'Dieppe beach under control, send in tanks.' He thought a moment, then wrote, 'All available landing-craft to Puys to evacuate wounded.' He looked sharply at the radio officer. 'You are fully aware of the situation on the beaches?'

'Yes, sir.'

'Good. Get the Intelligence officer and between you cook up some signals based on the present situation. Make it look favourable to the enemy so that he will send in anything else he has waiting out there.'

The man departed and the general looked at his watch. Eight o'clock. The battle had been in progress two and a half hours and except at Pourville the British had made no advance.

Just then the Chief of Staff came in. 'Bad news, sir. They have captured the Casino and some parties have penetrated into the town, but only small numbers.'

The general smiled. 'My signal has anticipated the event – they will try to reinforce that part of the beach, if they have any reserves in hand. Order the artillery to concentrate on the western section of the front and prepare for further landings.'

A signals-officer came in with a message from Berneval reporting that the enemy had withdrawn from the vicinity of the battery and were seen embarking from Belleville in one landing-craft. The battery had now opened barrage fire.

The general snorted. 'One landing-craft – say thirty men – have terrorized those German soldiers for the last two hours and then got away. My God!'

He controlled himself with an effort and turned to the Luftwaffe officer who had approached, looking pleased with himself. 'Our fighters are now in action, sir, attacking the enemy shipping and aircraft.'

The general growled: 'About time, don't you think?' He picked up his phone and talked for a long time to Dieppe, noticing as he spoke that the flag on the map before him had not been moved for some time. Finishing his conversation, he pointed to the flag without speaking.

'Yes, sir, they've halted at Appeville,' said the Chief of Staff.

The general glanced quickly through the sheaf of reports on his desk, then raising his voice addressed the room.

'Your attention, gentlemen.' There was silence. The officers gathered round and the general spoke. 'I want to put you all in the picture as it appears now. On the right flank all attacks have broken down on the beaches, all our defences are intact and reinforcements are available near by, consisting of the Anti-Tank Regiment and the Divisional Reserve. In the centre, at Dieppe, the enemy is trapped on beach. Some twenty-eight tanks landed have been destroyed and only a few small groups of the enemy have penetrated into the town. These have been dealt with but managed to do some damage to installations. The Casino has unfortunately been taken and is still being held by the enemy. Some of our machine-gun positions have been destroyed by shell-fire and our ack-ack batteries have been badly knocked about, but our artillery and mortars are largely intact. I expect a further landing in the vicinity of the Casino, but we are ready to receive it. At Pourville we are slowly driving the enemy back into the sea. I have reinforced this sector, as they will try to hold Pourville open to allow the inland force to escape. This force had halted and will soon commence its retreat. At Varengeville our battery there has been destroyed and all the personnel have been killed or captured. Our Air Force are attacking the ships and landing-craft, and I expect bomber attacks to commence at about eleven hours.'

He paused as an officer came in with a message. He read it slowly then said, 'The enemy has just attempted to reinforce the Dieppe beach, but has been driven off. Four craft got ashore and have been destroyed, together with all in them.'

A little sigh went up from the audience. Many of them could visualize the scene on Dieppe beach at that moment – the light vessels reeling and shuddering beneath the heavy shells, the shingle erupting in flame and smoke, the men torn and rent by flying steel, blood and guts and riven flesh everywhere.

But the general was speaking again. 'The battle is not yet over. There may be further attempts to reinforce the beaches, although our aircraft have not been able to find any large concentration of shipping elsewhere. That is all, gentlemen.'

At 8.30. G.II.Q. West telephoned to say that a tank division from Amiens was on the move towards Dieppe and should arrive about two o'clock. An S.S. Division had been alerted and was ready in case of a break-through. The general smiled: in spite of his favourable reports G.H.Q. were not taking any chances. Unless the British had something up their sleeves, the battle appeared to be won. Perhaps G.H.Q. knew something – paratroops perhaps, or a large fleet just now leaving England. Well, the next few hours would tell, and he had enough on his hands now to prevent the invaders escaping, if that was what they were thinking of. Anti-invasion measures had been taken and no more could be done. The next move lay with the enemy – withdraw or attack.

By 9.30 there was little change in the over-all situation. The battalion aiming at the airfield was now withdrawing towards Pourville, which still resisted strongly, although the British had been driven off the high ground at the western end of the beach. Every available man and weapon in that sector had been thrown into the battle in an all-out effort to destroy the invaders before they could re-embark, but the British were holding on stubbornly to every inch of ground in a desperate effort to keep open their line of escape. About this time a message came in from Dieppe to say that some prisoners had been taken. They were in possession of leaflets addressed to the French populace warning them to stay indoors, as the action was only a raid and not the invasion. This news was received with disbelief at Divisional H.Q. The general summed up the feeling of the staff when he said, 'They would never throw away twenty-eight tanks on a mere raid – no, this was meant to be something bigger.'

The news from Dieppe was reassuring. No further landing

attempts had been made and the remaining attackers were still pinned down on the beach; the fire from seawards appeared to be slackening, but aerial attacks continued ferociously against all battery positions. Luftwaffe fighters were active, attacking ships at sea, and had reported seeing many vessels heading away from the French coast towards England. The right flank was quiet, although landing-craft had made several attempts to approach Puys, only to be driven off.

The general reviewed the dispositions of his troops and felt satisfied. With the arrival of artillery reinforcements a great number of weapons were now concentrated against the beaches at Dieppe and Pourville, and any attempt on the part of the enemy to land additional troops or to evacuate those already there must be fraught with the greatest hazard. There was always the possibility of a large parachute drop somewhere behind Dieppe, on the race-course perhaps. Such a move might alter the position drastically, but unless it could be backed up by further landings it could only be a desperate gamble. If anything of the sort was contemplated it would have to be effected soon, as the enemy must know that reinforcements would be on the move towards Dieppe. Already the 2nd Battalion of the 570th Infantry Regiment had moved into position on the north side of the Forêt D'Arques in readiness to deal with any such move.

Shortly after ten o'clock the radio monitors reported having picked up a message from the H.Q. ship to the troops ashore ordering them to prepare to evacuate. Landing-craft would approach the beach at eleven o'clock to take off the men, but heavy equipment would have to be abandoned.

'They've had enough,' the general grunted. 'But it could be a blind.' He turned to the Chief of Staff. 'At the first sign of ships approaching the coast we'll put down a barrage on the sea verges and the beaches. They will certainly use smoke, but the artillery must keep firing whether they can see their targets or not. I want the whole of that foreshore up to four hundred yards out to sea covered.'

A few minutes before eleven o'clock a message from Pourville reported enemy landing-craft approaching the beach under cover of heavy fire from two destroyers. The village itself was still resisting strongly and so far had defied all German attacks, but it was evident that the enemy were preparing to retreat. This was followed by a signal from Dieppe advising that a smoke-screen had been laid over the whole of the beach. Persistent air-attacks were being launched against all gun-positions, but the batteries were still unharmed. Was it evacuation or a further landing? Well, the next thirty minutes would decide that. From the north-west came a steady thunder of gun-fire, perceptibly growing in volume from minute to minute. The artillery of the whole army corps was concentrating its fire on the Dieppe beach. Surely nothing could live in such an inferno. The general, recalling his own experiences on the western front during the First World War, shuddered at the picture of what was even now happening on the beach a few miles away.

His train of thought was interrupted by an excited Chief of Staff. 'They are going,' he cried. 'They are pulling out. There are landing-craft all along the beach embarking men, but we can only get intermittent glimpses of them because of the smoke.' The Chief of Staff added, 'The last of the batteries from Corps has arrived and is in action. They were shot up by aircraft on the way in and lost some men.'

The general glanced at his watch: 11.30 a.m. The battle had been raging for more than six hours, but now it looked as though the worst was over. The 571st Regiment had had its baptism of fire and had come through successfully, raw recruits and all. He wondered about casualties: the force attacking Pourville had been roughly handled and he knew that the gun-sites on the West Hill were mostly out of action. Well, losses did not matter – the important thing was that the enemy had been defeated and all the months of work and worry building up their defences was now justified.

Messages continued to pour in reporting the capture of a large number of prisoners, mostly Canadians, and at 1.15 the news came that the rear-guard in the Casino had surrendered and that the whole of the beach at Dieppe was now under control. Orders were given to get the prisoners away quickly, and all positions were to be reinforced. It was disquieting that ammunition was running short. Some batteries had only a few rounds left, and it would be some hours before fresh supplies could be brought up. The Tank Division was ordered in to Dieppe – just in case the enemy followed up at night. Besides, the sight of a large number of tanks would show the French people that the Germans were well able to take care of any rash invaders.

At 4.30 p.m. news came that the defenders of Pourville had been captured – they had apparently held out until all ammunition was exhausted, and shortly after five o'clock the general sent a signal to Corps H.Q. reporting the end of all armed resistance. Having done this, he ordered his car and set out for Dieppe. The troops there were exultant, but the officers were worried at the shortage of ammunition. The general reassured them.

'They won't try it this way again and the munitions will be here tonight. Do you gentlemen realize that you have shot off four weeks' supply in only six hours?' He laughed. 'We are all going to be scolded for this.'

Already shoals of visitors were arriving to inspect the scene. Bemedalled generals rubbed shoulders with pressmen, photographers were everywhere, radio men with their gear making recordings, all impeding and upsetting the officers who were struggling to regroup their men, check on losses, reorganize the defensive positions and attend to all the myriad details which must be done. After having been but-tonholed for the sixth time, the Chief of Staff grumbled to the general: 'You'd think these bastards had spent the day sitting on their backsides, just out of range, waiting for the show to end, so that they could dash in and make a scoop.' Which of course was exactly what they had done.

The following day an important commission from Berlin arrived, questioning, interviewing and demanding full reports from everybody. The staff, already up to their eyes in work, were nearly driven mad by the necessity to be polite to these V.I.P.s. Later in the day Von Rundstedt, the Com-mander-in-Chief, himself arrived, complete with staff, and set out on a tour of the beaches. Afterwards, at a little cere-mony beside the wreck of the Casino he presented decor-ations to a number of Luftwaffe officers who had distinguished themselves in the aerial combats, and to the divisional commander he awarded a bar to the Iron Cross. No other decorations were awarded to the Army. There was a stunned silence as Von Rundstedt walked away to his car; the assembled officers glanced at each other, their faces flushed with anger. This was unbelievable. Everyone had thought that the general would get the Knights' Cross and that at least some members of his staff would have been decorated, in addition to various officers and other ranks whose conduct during the battle merited recognition. But there was nothing. Later, when the matter was mentioned to the Commander-in-Chief, he dismissed it airily by saying that the battle was too short and unimportant to warrant a wholesale distribution of medals. However, he must have relented, because a long time afterwards some decorations for the Army did come through.

The commission studying the action had some criticism of the Luftwaffe for their tardy appearance, especially when it was disclosed that most of the fighter pilots had been given the night off duty and were away from their quarters. Confronted with the order from Army H.Q. cancelling the alert, there was nothing they could do. The fact that the divisional commander had ignored the cancellation order had passed without comment, but as expected, the artillery were slated for using too much ammunition. However, on the whole the top brass were pleased with the conduct of the Army. The German losses of some 600 were considered high, but were attributed to the large number of untrained men in the ranks. Everybody was atonished at the excellent equipment of the Canadians and the high quality and quantity of the rations brought ashore or salvaged from the stranded vessels. A large amount of cigarettes was much appreciated by the rank and file.

Meanwhile there was much work for everyone. Telephone lines had to be restored, shell-damaged positions repaired, abandoned equipment collected and the beach area thoroughly cleaned up. A problem immediately arose in the removal of the tanks from the beach. Many of these were not badly damaged and when their tracks were repaired should be mobile once again, but they were so firmly embedded in the shingle that forward motion was impossible. Also, because of the tank-traps and concrete walls barring access to or from the sea front to vehicles, they could not be brought into the town. Eventually the problem was solved by loading them on to special barges and removing them by sea, a difficult task owing to their great weight. A find of special interest was a complete copy of the British battle plan, which revealed an intention to drop parachutists on to the race-course outside Dieppe during the later stages of the action.

The plan showed that the British had an intimate knowledge of the terrain, all gun-positions being marked and even the presence of walls and ditches being indicated. A paragraph ordering that prisoners were to have their hands bound to prevent them from destroying their papers caused some resentment amongst the staff. It was known that some soldiers being taken from the beach at Pourville had escaped when the landing-craft in which they had been placed was sunk. On being interrogated these men confirmed that their hands had been tied while on shore, but once on the vessel they were freed. Later, when the news came that the Canadian prisoners had been shackled as a reprisal, the general and most of his staff were horrified. They were professional soldiers and as such felt no bitterness towards the enemy – the maltreatment of prisoners offended all their traditions.

The High Command formed the opinion that the attack was an invasion spearhead and that any success at Dieppe would have been immediately exploited. The captured battle plan gave detailed instructions and times for evacuation, but it was pointed out that these could have been amended at any time during the action, if the situation warranted a change. They strongly criticized the plan as a whole, for its inflexibility, lack of artillery support and preliminary bombardment, and summed up by declaring that it appeared to have been framed in a theoretical manner reflecting inexperience of battle.

To the Germans the outstanding lesson of the Dieppe affair was to confirm that any invasion attempt could be stopped on the beaches. Hitler himself said that the one regiment at Dieppe had done what it would have taken three divisions to do if the attackers had succeeded in penetrating any distance inland. From that time on, even greater effort was made to develop a belt of fortifications along the whole of the west coast, strong enough to break any assault, wherever it might fall. Special attention was given to fortifying the neighbourhood of seaports. The defences had to be of a strength capable of resisting the heaviest naval and air bombardment. In their obsession with the West Wall, defence in depth was neglected or thought unnecessary. This work was pushed ahead with the utmost speed, spurred on by persistent reports from German agents in Britain of troop concentrations in South of England ports. Many of

Hitler's crack divisions were brought up to reinforce the coastal areas of Normandy during the early autumn of 1942, and with all German effort and thought focused on the West Wall, on 8th November came invasion. Not, however, in France but in North Africa.

This turn-up resulted in Hitler's occupying Vichy France, but caused no relaxation of effort on the west coast. Somewhere here would come the final blow. That it would come nobody had any doubt, and that it would strike at a seaport was equally certain. Apparently it never occurred to Hitler or his advisers that next time the enemy came he would bring his own port with him.

Information

IF we consider this operation to be what it purported to be, a raid that had to look like an invasion, we can see that it presented a peculiarly difficult problem to the Public Relations Department of Combined Operations H.Q. and one which, in the event, they were unable to cope with.

The problem came under two heads: (a) for the first time Allied troops were joined in combat with the Germans; and (b) following hard on the heels of Mr Molotov's visits to London and Washington and Mr. Churchill's trip to Moscow, news of which was released only on 18th August, the raid, if raid it was, would be wide open to misrepresentation and misunderstanding.

To the world it would appear to be the long-awaited second front, and it was a foregone conclusion that the Germans would play up the invasion theory to the utmost. Whatever happened at Dieppe, the enemy was being given a golden opportunity to claim that he had thwarted an attempt at invasion. This was fully appreciated at Combined Operations H.Q., as were the possible repercussions overseas when it was learnt that Canadian and American soldiers had participated. Enormous interest would immediately be aroused across the Atlantic, more especially in America, as this would be the first occasion that U.S. troops had been in action against the Germans in the war. The task before the Public Relations people was to squash from the outset any attempt by the enemy to represent the raid as an invasion, and secondly to ensure that the roles of the mixed forces engaged would be clearly defined, so that there could be no misapprehension in Canada and America about the parts played by their respective armies. In order to fulfil these necessary requirements and to keep the initiative in the anticipated propaganda battle, a steady flow of unequivocal communiqués was indicated.

There appears to have been some muddled thinking about the desirability of mentioning the participation of American troops in the action. In view of the infinitesimal part they would take, it might have been better to have said nothing about them, but once it was decided to mention them, why not have stated outright that only fifty Rangers had come along for the experience? Instead, in the earlier communiqués, no numbers were given, and this error of judgment was to have unfortunate results, as we shall see.

The first news of the affair came at 6.15 a.m. on the 19th in a broadcast from London to the people of Dieppe, telling them the attack was not the invasion but only a raid. They were to stay in their homes and take no part in the fighting. All over the world wires immediately began to hum, and newspaper editors sharpened their pencils in anticipation of big news. But alas, there was no news, at least none from London – not until late in the evening, when a second communiqué was issued, stating that heavy fighting was in progress and that the attacking force comprised mainly Canadians, with a detachment of Americans, some Commandos and tanks. This message was obviously very much delayed before reaching the newspapers and the B.B.C. So it went on. Vague, uninformative announcements, with long intervals between, were reluctantly issued by Combined Operations H.Q. Their very vagueness made them suspect, and editors were quick to detect that something was being concealed. Frantic for a story, the newspapers seized upon the only definite information available to them, the Commando success at Quiberville, and headlined the raid as a Commando operation, excluding all mention of the Canadian part, about which they had practically no details. To make matters worse, the American papers came out with the claim that the raid was an American show, in spite of having been informed through their Army H.Q. in London that only fifty U.S. soldiers took part. While there might be some small excuse for the line adopted by the British Press, the American attitude was inexcusable. It was yellow journalism at its worst.

Some efforts were apparently made by Combined Operations H.Q. to put the venture in its proper perspective, but the Press on both sides of the Atlantic were off at a gallop on their chosen courses, and nothing could stop them. The result of all this was to give to the world a completely false picture of the Dieppe raid, one which greatly upset the Canadian public, who, being better served by their Press, had learnt that Canadian troops had been heavily engaged in the battle. These were, of course, only domestic troubles, and while always liable to upset relations between the three countries concerned, if only temporarily, were not very serious. However, a greater threat was beginning to emerge in the German propaganda, which had been taking full advantage of the lack of clear statements from London to fill the air with eye-witness accounts and official comments. After a quiet start their propaganda machine got into top gear, the principal line of attack being that the British had been forced into a hasty and badly organized invasion attempt by pressure from Russia. This theory was pressed home by the enemy over a period of some weeks, and with the seed of doubt already planted in people's minds it is little wonder that the Dieppe raid came to be regarded both at home and abroad as an invasion attempt which had met a deserved and bloody ending. British propaganda had simply no answer to the German attack, except to repeat on a couple of occasions that the affair was a raid and not an invasion. The disclosure of the objectives of the raid, on 21st August, as a test of German defences and the destruction of batteries and a radar station, did nothing to allay public disquiet. If German reports were true, the British had lost heavily in men and equipment, losses out of all proportion to the things achieved. And people turning to London for comfort and information found none.

From the viewpoint of propaganda, there can be no doubt that the raid took place at the worst possible time, and, however it ended, was certain to present the Germans with a powerful weapon to use against us. Ending as it did in an entirely unexpected disaster left the military authorities in an awkward position. C.O.H.Q. were unable to explain away the operation in a convincing manner and equally unable to control the home and overseas Press. Some of the blame for the unfortunate situation which developed can be laid at the door of an over-strict censorship, and some attributed to the pre-arranged policy of C.O.H.Q. to play down the operation. In addition, the Ministry of Information displayed a lack of imagination in the always difficult matter of apportioning publicity between the components of an international force. This fault was the direct cause of many of the misconceptions which arose. For example, a Private and Confidential Memo to Editors, released on the afternoon of the 19th, stated: 'For your own information I may say that while Canadian troops comprise the main body of the raiding force, they constitute approximately one-third of the total personnel of all services participating in the raid.' With no idea of the composition of the striking force, what could the public make of that item?

So, in a dilemma, C.O.H.Q. took refuge under a cloak of secrecy which went beyond the dictates of security and which, in the long run, did more harm than good.

Of course, security had to be considered, but no great injury to the war effort could have resulted from mentioning in the earlier communiqués that the operation had as its main objective the garnering of experience for the future. This would have explained the use of tanks and the large number of troops involved, which seemed out of keeping with a hit-and-run raid. It would not have told the Germans anything useful – when they studied the action they would realize that it could have been an experimental raid. They knew all about our casualties, they had all our equipment, and they had a copy of the battle plan to tell them anything else they wanted to know. A clear disclosure of the motive in the early stages would have stolen much of their thunder.

As it was, to the British public and the world, Dieppe remained an enigma. Raid or invasion? Who could tell?

Now that once top-secret documents have been made available to the historians, it can be said that there appears to be not a shred of evidence in support of the invasion theory. In itself this might not be conclusive, as it was found that Operation 'Jubilee' was very poorly documented, probably for security reasons, and this might equally apply if there had been a last-minute decision to exploit any success at Dieppe. However, in view of the British Government's decision of July 1942, not to stage an invasion that year, we may be reasonably certain that there was no such decision.

Of course, the Germans believed otherwise, and apart from their propaganda they had some reason to do so. From their records, it appears that around nine o'clock on the morning of the battle, their reconnaissance planes reported spotting a convoy of twenty-six ships with decks packed with troops off the south coast of England. This report caused G.H.Q. West to order a general alert for all forces in Normandy and Brittany, as it was believed this was the invasion fleet en route for Dieppe. It is now said that this report was inaccurate, and that what the German pilot saw was a routine convoy of fourteen merchant ships bound for the Isle of Wight. Later, the German Navy Operations Staff, who investigated the matter, stated that their radar intelligence had picked up a convoy of twenty-six merchant ships, eastbound, near the approximate area of sighting. Whatever the truth, by this time the invasion theory was so popular with the German High Command that many officers who did not agree with it did not dare to put forward contradicting theories.

It must be remembered that Operation 'Jubilee' set out to give the appearance of invasion, and this it certainly succeeded in doing, the large number of tanks engaged being particularly convincing to the enemy.

Should there be still lingering doubts about the affair, let us see whether a study of the composition of the striking force provides any help. Were the dispositions and equipment of the troops consistent with the requirements of an invasion spearhead? I think they were. Backed by sixty tanks and supported by a detachment of artillerymen who went ashore at Puys to man captured batteries, the force was sufficiently powerful to hold the proposed Dieppe perimeter long enough to enable reinforcements and heavy equipment to be landed. Certainly their ability to do so depended on seizing the town without sustaining heavy casualties, and on enemy troop movements to the area being as slow as had been anticipated. In other words, had the landings gone according to plan, then the way was open for invasion.

Apart from this one factor, nothing else in the plan suggests an intention to exploit. The two large groups of Commandos were to be sent home after completing their missions on the flanks, which would hardly have been the case if an invasion had been intended.

There were no heavy air-attacks on rail and road communications, nor on the advancing German reinforcements, who, except for isolated fighter attacks, were unmolested. Except for a raid on Abbeville airfield, all air action was directed against targets in and around Dieppe.

Finally, apart from the mysterious 26-ship convoy, no other assembly of shipping was reported by the Luftwaffe, nor are the alleged landing attempts on other parts of the coast mentioned in German Army records. These were figments of the propaganda machine and may be disregarded.

The weight of evidence is against the invasion theory. 'Jubilee' was a raid, nothing more, an action which can take its place alongside the Charge of the Light Brigade as an example of the stupidity, wastefulness and heroism of war.

Not the least fascinating aspect of Operation 'Jubilee' was the work of the Intelligence and Security Departments, which had to cover an astonishingly wide field. This comes broadly under two headings – information about the enemy and keeping him from learning of our intention to attack.

As mentioned elsewhere, the whole area of Dieppe was minutely photographed from the air, and every detectable gun-site, pillbox, trench and so on, pin-pointed. In addition, the coast was photographed from a very low level during nautical twilight and in daylight, to show the beaches and cliffs behind them in silhouette, exactly as they would appear to the navigators of approaching vessels.

All possible information about the number of enemy troops in the area, state of training, position of reserves and speed of reinforcement was collected and studied.

Afterwards the Germans expressed surprise at the amount of detailed information we had about their defence system, but pointed out that while all their fixed positions had been located, very little was known about what was concealed inside. This was only too true and would appear to indicate that our Intelligence service in the area of assault was, at that time, somewhat sketchy. Nothing was known about the 75s in the caves or the guns on the Promenade which only appeared at night. The number of troops in the front line was greatly underestimated, and the transfer of German Divisional H.Q. to Enverme, which had taken place months before, had passed unnoticed. It is perhaps significant that the situation maps at Army H.Q. in Berlin (O.K.H.) still placed the Divisional H.Q. at Arques as late as mid-August. One might assume from this fact that most of the information about Dieppe not originating from aerial reconnaissance came from agents in Berlin. The error in stating that the 110th Division was in Dieppe instead of the 302nd was curious, and has never been explained. Examination of German records showed that the 110th had never been in France but had spent the war years on the Russian front.

Of course, the gathering of information about the enemy on the French coast by on-the-spot agents must have been incredibly difficult. The beach areas were sealed off, and every town and village had its quota of counter-espionage personnel – spying on the troops and the local people, sitting in cafés with their ears pricked. Woe betide any German soldier who, in his cups, said the wrong thing, and woe betide any French people who might have overheard him.

Apart altogether from the garnering of information about the enemy, the security angle at home had to be considered. The big headache for the authorities arose because of the cancellation of Operation 'Rutter' in July, after everybody had been thoroughly briefed, and there were several cases of security breaches by members of the forces concerned. In England, as in France, members of the security forces sat around in public places with pricked ears, listening for foolish talk. But this was only part of the task confronting M.I.5. The assembling, training and equipping of a large expedition immediately gave rise to a multitude of security problems. Not only was the movement of the troops likely to cause speculation, but the vast quantity of equipment required would certainly cause talk. Guns, ammunition and a thousand and one items, ranging from folding parachutist bicycles (for the Camerons) to firemen's axes and waterproofing material for tanks, had to be drawn from various sources. Any large demand for a particular article might raise curiosity. There were the usual inter-service difficulties in meeting requisitions, some of them unusual, and the inevitable crop of busybodies at the depots who demanded to know for what purpose the equipment was needed before parting with it. All these problems had to be dealt with in a natural, everyday manner – no special pressure could be brought to bear on any particularly sticky depot. Then there was the problem of delivery. The simple way was to send everything to one central point, but this could not be done, so the stores had to be distributed over a large number of points whence they would be collected by the various units concerned. This dispersal was a feat of organization in itself, but like all the other difficulties was met and overcome by the Security people. No doubt many suspicions that something was in the wind were aroused, but as we know, nothing leaked out. Security was preserved until the end, a notable achievement under the circumstances.

Evaluation

THE retention of Dieppe as the target for a second attempt was greatly critized at the time. It had been done against the advice of some, at least, of the Army Commanders, and there was a distinct atmosphere of 'I told you so' prevalent at H.Q. afterwards.

The decision was in the nature of a gamble, it being thought that even if the enemy had learnt of the abortive attempt in July, he would never expect another attack so soon on the same place. An alternative destination had been discussed, but with the invasion season drawing to a close, there was simply not time enough to reconnoitre a fresh area properly.

If there was to be a raid at all, it must be on Dieppe. It was either cancel or proceed – and nobody wanted to cancel, at least nobody at Combined Operations H.Q.

When the battered ships returned to England with their cargoes of wounded and exhausted men, it must have appeared to the planners that their gamble had failed.

The question was then, Did the brush with the German convoy give the game away, or had there been a security leak? Of course, there was no way of knowing, and the naval engagement seemed the obvious explanation of the disaster, and was generally accepted as such, until the battle reports were studied, when the authorities must have been in some confusion of mind as to the true cause.

These reports showed that almost complete surprise was achieved on the right flank, therefore the enemy cannot have been in the state of alert which one would expect if he had been forewarned. On the other hand, the tremendous fire-power brought to bear on the Dieppe beach far exceeded anything anticipated, and might indicate that he had got wind of the coming assault. There was one other explanation, of course: that intelligence reports and estimates of the defences were at fault.

Of those put ashore at Dieppe and Puys, only one senior officer returned, and he was wounded at the moment of landing, so that it was impossible for the authorities to piece together a clear picture of the battle.

One fact emerged, however: every survivor of the holocaust on those beaches was convinced that the enemy was forewarned. That they should have thought so is not altogether surprising. They point out that after weeks spent at practice embarkations and landings, always under cover of darkness or smoke, they were embarked in broad daylight on the 18th, with no smoke-cover and with rumours circulating of German aircraft in some areas. The very fact that Dieppe being the target again was disquieting, and as their briefing had given them no idea at all of the fire-power they were to encounter on the beaches, it is little wonder that they formed the conclusion that their arrival was expected.

Not until long after the war was the truth known, when examination of German records revealed that the High Command had no knowledge of the proposed attack on 8th July. Apparently enemy Intelligence attached no significance to the reported gathering of ships off the Isle of Wight on that date, and no news had leaked out of England. We also know that he had no warning of the troop embarkations on 18th August. This is borne out by the War Diary of the 302nd Division, then in Dieppe, which records the receipt of an order from Army H.Q. on the 18th, cancelling the alert as from that night. The divisional commander did not obey this order, not because he had any inkling of trouble, but merely because he thought the cancellation premature. The Luftwaffe, however, stood down, and most of the pilots were away on night leave until early on the 19th.

The German records also disclose that the naval battle in the small hours attracted no particular attention ashore, but it seems that some, at least, of the garrison at Puys and Berneval went to their posts, although the general alarm was not sounded until 5 a.m. when the landings on the right flank were going in. This is remarkable when we remember that the flotilla bearing the Royal Regiment to Puys had been illuminated by either flares or a searchlight, or both, for the best part of an hour.

As we mention elsewhere, the German troops in the Dieppe area and probably everywhere along the coast had been kept in the highest state of readiness during the danger periods, and on the night of 18–19th August were in the normal condition of alert. No unusual defensive measures were taken, and those men not on duty undressed and went to bed.

It is true that, a few days before, wild stories of British landings on various parts of the coast had begun to go the rounds and we know, from French sources, that the men were nervous and expectant, but this state of mind could be attributed to the effect of outside events and the long period of alert. There is no evidence to show that the Germans had any foreknowledge of the attack; in fact, quite the opposite.

The picture then, at fifteen minutes to five o'clock on the morning of 19th August shows a heavily defended coastline, with only some of the forward positions actually manned. There are look-outs and sentries aplenty, but conditions favour a surprise attack. It will take the enemy from five to ten minutes to bring all his posts into action, and then most of the fire will be on predicted lines, until targets can be established. The invaders must be off the beaches and attacking the enemy within that brief span. A difficult but not impossible task on the flanking beaches, but a very different matter on the main beach at Dieppe. Here, where surprise was of paramount importance, there was to be none. Instead, out of deference to the known heavy defences, there would be a brief bombardment from sea and air, under cover of which the troops would approach the beach and make their landing. This lack of surprise, combined with a gross under-estimation of the defences, brought about the downfall of the enterprise. The attack was literally smashed at the verge of the sea and never got properly under way.

There were other reasons contributing to the general failure – lack of artillery support, lack of flexibility, lack of proper communications – none of which would have mattered a lot if the vitally important element of surprise had been present at the start.

But there was to be no surprise. With success or failure hanging on a slender thread of time, the frontal assault was timed to go in half an hour after the flank attacks had awakened the whole district, and the enemy given a precious thirty minutes to rub the sleep from his eyes and get into position. One asks, why?

Some people thought that the times of high tide, which can vary considerably on quite adjacent beaches on this coast, had a bearing on the matter, but the official explanation is that there would not have been sufficient sea-room for all the craft involved if the three groups were approaching the flank and centre at the same time. Further, to produce the R.H.L.I. and the Essex Scottish off Dieppe at five o'clock would have entailed the troop-carriers leaving port half an hour earlier, in daylight, with risk of being spotted by the regular German reconnaissance planes. These are purely naval reasons, and while due respect must be paid to expert opinion, one would have thought that on a front eleven miles in length by ten miles in depth there would have been ample room for 237 vessels, not all of which would be approaching the beach at the same time. This gives about one square mile for every two ships. If we consider the flotilla destined for Dieppe, consisting of three infantry landing-ships carrying the R.H.L.I. and Essex Scottish, totalling, with attached units about 1,200 men, it will be seen that some forty assault boats would be required to put this force ashore.

With the three tank landing-craft which should have accompanied them, plus sundry motor boats and support landing-craft, we have a total of about sixty vessels coming in to a beach one mile in length. Sailing remember, in close company over a sea area of ten square miles. Surely the Navy was being over-fussy about sea-room?*

So far as an earlier start was concerned, it is a fact that the nine infantry landing-ships actually left port before dark. They had been disguised to resemble merchant ships to an extent which would render recognition of their true character impossible in the evening light. Even had it been necessary to leave half an hour earlier – which it wasn't – where lay the greater risk? To be early at the start or late at the end?

The nine L.S.I.s, like all other craft in the fleet, had plenty

* On D-Day over 5,000 ships approached a strip of coast about fifty miles wide and landed tens of thousands of troops on five beaches, the total width of which would be not more than twenty miles.

of time in hand, and they all arrived at their trans-shipment points at 3 a.m. Even the slower tank landing-craft were in their correct positions, with the three T.L.C.s of the first flight, which would land on the main beach with the infantry, not more than a mile or two behind the Red and White Beach force. The troops destined for Orange, Green and Blue Beaches were lowered away at once, but the Red and White contingent was not put into the water until 3.20 a.m. (Like the Royal Regiment this force suffered a delayed start, but notwithstanding were only three minutes late at Dieppe.) By 3.45 a.m. they were well on their way, with the three T.L.C.s only about one and a half miles astern. At this hour, their position would be about nine miles from the coast, which would give them plenty of time to touch down at or before five o'clock, complete with tanks. Instead, they were held back until 5.20 a.m. There seems no sense or reason for it.

With no surprise possible on the main beach, everything depended upon the preliminary bombardment to keep the Germans' heads down, and this it failed to do. The carefully reconnoitred Dieppe defences were unharmed and proved more than capable of breaking up the attack. In addition to the known gun-positions, there were many more weapons, especially mortars, ranged on the beach, indeed far more than anyone had anticipated. This extensive use of mortars was only one of the unpleasant surprises of the day; the anti-tank guns which appeared on the sea front during the hours of darkness were another, and the final blow was the presence of numerous 75s in the recesses of the two headlands. None of these decisive factors was known in advance; they could not be detected by aerial photography, but good Intelligence work might have helped. The Germans were surprised at the extent of our knowledge of their defences, but mentioned that very little was known as to what the fixed positions contained.

Our Intelligence reports seemed out of date. It was stated that the German 110th Division was in line, with headquarters at Arques-la-Bataille, while in fact the 302nd Division held the area and H.Q. had been at Envermu since the previous spring. In the event this did not matter, but one wonders if reports about the fixed defences were equally faulty.

The battle for Dieppe was lost in the first few minutes, when the assaulting battalions were cut to ribbons on the main beach, and the chain reaction of disaster set in from that time. With the emergence of the East Headland from its smoke-screen, doom was writ large across that expanse of torn stones and spouting water. What a pity that this hill, suspect always, was not treated with the respect it deserved as the unknown quantity and blotted out for a further period.

The attempt on Puys was pure tragedy. Half an hour late, and with the bulk of the regiment landing in daylight, the Royal Regiment went to their deaths. To press home the assault under such conditions was utter madness, yet their orders left them no alternative.

Apparently the delay suffered at the start-point was not known to those on *Calpe*, but even if they had been aware of it, there was nothing that could be done. Once the force had left the trans-shipment area they could not be recalled or diverted owing to the strict imposition of radio silence. To make matters worse, in an effort to make up lost time, a high speed was maintained on the run-in, in consequence of which many vessels fell behind through lack of power and the pre-arranged order of landing was upset. But this probably did not matter; surprise was lost and with it went their main weapon. Radios could not be used to report their position until after 5.20 a.m., by which time most of the signallers were dead on the beach and those who survived were unable to make contact with *Calpe*. The first signal to get through was that at 6.40 a.m., reporting failure to land. Where this mysterious message originated nobody can tell, but it may well have come from the solitary landing-craft which pulled off Blue Beach without disembarking her complement. If so, it was sadly misinterpreted in *Calpe*'s wireless-room. The satisfaction engendered by the naval flotilla commander's news of a successful landing was soon dissipated by the signal at 7.30 a.m. asking to be taken off. What had happened at Blue Beach? Nobody knew.

These incidents serve to illustrate the difficulties under which General Roberts had to labour. His was an almost impossible task owing to the breakdown in communications between the forces ashore and the H.Q. ship. The naval signals-party put ashore at Dieppe were all killed or wounded in the first few minutes and all Army radio sets brought ashore were out of action, except for an '18' set on Red Beach and a scout car set on White Beach. Through this latter apparatus Brigadier Southam kept in touch with the H.Q. ship throughout the day. He had little enough to report, pinned down as he was under the wall for most of the action, but many of his signals cannot have reached the Force Commander on *Calpe*, as the desperate position on the Dieppe beach does not appear to have been appreciated by H.Q. until late in the day.

There was no shortage of signals being received in *Calpe*'s operations-room, most of them from enemy sources, and such was the congestion and confusion there that genuine requests from the shore for special tasks, such as smoke-laying, were greatly delayed in transit.

The almost total lack of information from the battlefields left the force commander completely in the dark about events ashore. Visual observation was impossible because of the smoke that shrouded the whole coast, and at no time had he a true picture of the situation. During the morning he received two signals from the main beach, which led him to a course of action serving only to magnify the tragedy taking place on shore. The first was the distorted message from Red Beach reporting progress into the town, and the other from White Beach reporting the fall of the Casino and stating the beach was under control. These incorrect messages caused General Roberts to send in his reserves to support Red and White Beaches, with the results we already know. Under the circumstances it was the only possible decision to take, obsessed as all were with the urgent need to silence one or both of the headlands.

The Pourville action can best be described as a near miss. It almost, but not quite, came off. Certainly surprise was achieved, in spite of landing ten minutes after the party began at Quiberville, and the assault troops eased the way for their comrades following close behind. Even the Camerons, who were late, got off the beach without much difficulty, although not without a warm welcome from the enemy. However, the first hurdle was safely negotiated, but from then on, there was trouble. The Dieppe perimeter defence proved impregnable to lightly-armed infantry, and there were simply not enough men available to hold the enemy off the beach and keep a safe escape-corridor open. The Camerons were set the difficult task of advancing some miles inland across hostile territory, capturing the airfield at St. Aubyn, in conjunction with the tanks from Dieppe, and then moving farther on to take the German Divisional H.Q. at Arques-la-Bataille. Having accomplished their mission, they would retire to Dieppe for evacuation, with the possibility of having to fight every foot of the way back. All this in the space of four hours. Actually, had they succeeded in reaching Arques they would have searched in vain for the German H.Q. which had been removed to Envermu, on the far side of the Forêt D'Arques, since the previous February. As it happened, the Camerons did not encounter much opposition either going or coming, and were able to move with speed in each direction. But theirs was wasted effort – they had little chance to damage the enemy until the rear-guard action at Pourville, and would have been more usefully employed in supporting the South Sasks in the attacks on the Dieppe perimeter. A breakthrough here would have enabled the two regiments to overrun the West Headland and brought immeasurable relief to the hard-pressed troops on the main beach. The proposed seizure of the airfield seems over-ambitious for what was to all intents and purposes a large-scale raid. One wonders if there was some deeper intent here, the landing of airborne forces, maybe.

As to the Commando landings on the extreme flanks, one was completely successful and the other a complete failure – a failure illuminated by the deeds of the small group who terrorized the German battery for the best part of two hours.

The breakdown in communications between shore and ship which so bedevilled the operation was largely occasioned by the heavy casualties suffered by the signalling parties who went ashore and by damage to, or loss of, their equipment.

For the operation, *Calpe* and *Fernie* were draped with extra radio antennae, and no less than thirty-two wireless transmitters, receivers and radio navigational aid sets were installed in the two ships, neither of which could fire their four-inch guns for fear of upsetting the delicate equipment, and did not do so until the end of the day.

Some sixty additional personnel were embarked to operate

the sets, which would provide communication between the Headquarters ships and England, all ships in the force, naval shore-parties, military units ashore and afloat, and all aircraft operating in the area.

The operators were drawn from the three Services, and to ensure the smooth running of the complicated system much joint practice and training was indicated. Unfortunately, for security reasons, it was not possible to collect together the various elements for rehearsals under the one roof. Each of the three Services trained independently – a fundamentally bad arrangement for a combined operation. A further factor militating against efficiency was the lack of space available on the destroyers which prevented a proper layout of the equipment. In spite of these handicaps, however, no serious failure of communications occurred, in so far as the H.Q. ships were concerned. Certainly some important messages were not received, for reasons unknown, and others from enemy sources were accepted, chiefly because many of the signals passed to *Calpe* were in plain language and not in code. Bad W/T discipline on the part of the force as a whole, plus the German efforts, caused much congestion and confusion in *Calpe*, but when the difficulties of working a highly complex system of communications under the existing conditions are considered, it will be appreciated that the signallers did a remarkable job of work.

Operation 'Jubilee' posed two questions: was it really necessary, and if so, could it not have been done in some other and less costly manner? The answer to the first question must be, Yes. From both the political and military angles some such enterprise was important, not only to fulfil our promise to Russia, but also with an eye to the immensely greater undertaking that lay ahead. One cannot quarrel with that – it is not so much the deed as the manner of its doing that can be faulted.

To the second question one must also give an affirmative answer. It could have been done in a different way.

We have already pointed out how the absence of a preliminary bombardment, allied to bad timing of the frontal assault, brought about a condition of stalemate at Dieppe. The decision to dispense with the bombardment is peculiar, although there were seemingly good reasons for doing so, just as there were for discarding the plan to stage the main

148

attacks on the flanks. The high-level bombing was dropped because the R.A.F. said they could not guarantee to hit the small targets on the sea front, and the Army feared that the resultant damage to the town would prevent the tanks from getting through. Also a heavy bombing attack would serve to alert the enemy. Do these reasons really stand up to examination? Could not accuracy of bombing have been secured by pathfinders dropping flares over the target area? Would the debris in the streets have proved a worse obstacle to the tanks than the undamaged concrete walls? Could not a few raids have been made on other coastal ports during the preceding nights, so persuading the Germans that the bombing attack on Dieppe was part of a general programme?

Then the decision to proceed with the frontal attack without a preliminary bombardment seems suicidal, but one can understand how the planners were tempted by the prospect of bringing the attackers smack into the main objective without any loss of time. It was really a question as to where lay the greater danger: to risk landing the tanks on the far side of two rivers, six miles from their objective, or go all out for the centre.

So far as river crossings are concerned, bridges can always be secured and held, a job dear to the hearts of Commandos, and it should have been possible to ascertain whether the bridges were capable of carrying the heavy tanks. Some of the tanks might have been put ashore at Pourville, to the east of the River Scie, but apparently there was some doubt as to their ability to get off the beach through the only available exit. The main road to Dieppe runs very close to the beach at this point, and one wonders why this possibility was not more fully explored. One must admit that the choice was not an easy one, and in the upshot the wrong decision was taken, in a spirit of supreme optimism. Once committed to the frontal assault, why deprive the troops of their principal weapon – surprise?

It was impossible to have the whole force on the beach before 5.20, why not have sent in one battalion to spearhead the landings, as at Pourville? Or better still, use a strong force of Commandos to land before five o'clock and thus tie in with the flank attacks. Of course, Dieppe beach was a very different proposition from Pourville, but 400 or 500 Commandos, achieving all possible surprise, would certainly have dealt with the defences in the immediate front and much of the West Hill, and so opened the way for a quick follow-up by the Canadians. This seems an ideal task for Commandos, with their special qualities of mobility and flexibility, qualities not usually found in infantry, who are trained to act in groups – section, platoon or company, as the case may be.

Let it not be thought that this implies any criticism of the Canadian effort. They were highly-trained troops, ready and anxious to get to grips with the enemy. There was great pride in them at having been chosen for this rather desperate venture, and every man was fully determined to give a good account of himself. In the event their hopes were dashed, their brave endeavours in vain. It was not their fault, they were the victims of miscalculation and mistake.

Combined Operations Headquarters claimed that tactical surprise had been achieved, and blamed the failure at Dieppe not on bad timing, but on the troops' being held up short of the wall by wire which proved much heavier than anticipated. With no tanks to smash a way through, the men were caught in the open while struggling to cut the wire. This is true enough, but it must be remembered that the assault parties were not solely depending on the tanks to breach the wire. They were accompanied ashore by sappers with the necessary equipment to blow gaps in the fence, and the sappers, like so many of the assault force, were slaughtered at the very edge of the sea. This viewpoint quite overlooked the fact that the Germans, who should have been asleep in their beds, were wide awake and sitting behind their guns, waiting. Indeed, even if the wire had been light or non-existent, it is very doubtful whether the result would have been any different. The Germans had prepared their predicted lines of fire in such a way that some guns fired on craft approaching the shore, some on the water's edge to catch the men as they left their boats, some enfiladed the beach and others swept the 150 yards of open space between the sea wall and the buildings inland.

Disorganized and confused as they were after landing, it seems unlikely that the Canadians could have progressed far beyond the wall in face of the storm of fire let loose upon them.

The enemy, who never believed in sending a boy to do a man's job, were surprised that the British should have thought it possible to overcome their defences with the light armaments employed. They pointed out that seemingly too much reliance was placed on the ability of cannon-fighters and small naval guns to cow the defenders, safe behind feet-thick concrete. When it is realized that the normal requirements of a brigade in land warfare (at that time), attacking on a 2,000-yard front, would be 140 guns, ranging from light infantry support weapons to heavy howitzers for counter-battery work, it will be seen how poor was the artillery support at Dieppe, where the heaviest guns were of four-inch calibre – and there were not many of them.

One of the mysteries of the affair is why the plan was permitted to go through after the removal of the bombardment, the one real safety factor in the frontal assault. One would have expected that with such a vital change being made the whole plan would have been examined afresh, and either strengthened or cancelled out of hand. To strengthen it without using bombers meant the inclusion of a cruiser or battleship to give the necessary fire-support – something which the Admiralty simply would not hear of, because of the risk of operating a capital ship in the narrow waters of the Channel. To cancel seemed equally out of the question. 'Jubilee' must take place, come hell or high water.

With no bombardment and no artillery support, surely a simple alteration in the timing of the frontal assault would have made all the difference between failure and success. This thirty-minute delay was a hang-over from the original plan, which envisaged the defences stunned and bewildered after a heavy bombing. With this eliminated, zero hour on the main beach should have been brought forward to co-incide with the flank landings, and there seems to be no valid reason for not doing so.

As we have mentioned already, the 'Jubilee' plan was the work of the Planning Staff of Combined Operations Headquarters, in conjunction with representatives of Home Forces H.Q. The Combined Operations people produced the plan for attack from the flanks, while the Home Forces staff wanted a frontal attack – and got their way. Both the outline plan, which included a bombardment, and the detailed plan, which did not, would be submitted to the Army Chiefs of Staff for approval or otherwise. The dropping of the bombardment was apparently a unanimous decision of all aparties, who in the end succeeded in hatching out a regular hermaphorite – neither one thing nor the other.

It has been said authoritatively that the plan suffered because too many people had a hand in the making, and certainly, apart from the faults mentioned above, there were other things which merit criticism. It was over-optimistic, over-ambitious and too rigid. The first two were undoubtedly the result of an incorrect appreciation of the enemy's strength and mobility; the last to some extent was unavoidable. In any military operation involving attacks on a wide front flexibility of control and movement is essential, so that units may be switched from point to point as the situation demands. Owing to the lack of training of the naval crews, such flexibility at Dieppe was not possible, and, if exercised, could have made the disaster more complete. Also, with the failure of shore-to-ship communications, control over the land forces was precluded, and even had such control existed, there was little the force commander could have done, once the troops were committed to the beaches. As we have seen, it proved extremely difficult, if not impossible, to withdraw. About a half of the Pourville force were taken off, less than one-fifth from Dieppe and none from Puys. Conditions on the beaches prevented any switching of units, but if the force commander had been aware of these conditions, he might have been able to use some initiative in his handling of the reserves. Instead of throwing them away on the main beach – reinforcing weakness – they could have been landed at Pourville for a flank attack on Dieppe, thus exploiting the one successful landing.

The inherent weakness of the plan lay in the absolute necessity of all the landings succeeding – any failure of one was likely to prejudice all the others.

Some alternative courses were provided for in the plan to cover the possible loss of certain of the infantry landing-ships at sea. For example, if the South Saskatchewan Regiment had been lost, the Camerons would have taken over the task of securing Pourville and abandoned the attempt on the airfield. It seems quite clear that, notwithstanding any such loss, the military intended to proceed with the venture, but the naval force commander took the sensible precaution of placing on record his intention to abandon the expedition if one or more of the larger landing-ships was sunk en route.

The question, Could it have been done differently? and the affirmative answer thereto, beget another question, Why then was it not done in some other manner? As we have shown, there were reasons for not using bombers, and against the flank attacks, however doubtful they may seem, just as there were for lack of artillery support. The answer to the question must be sought in the military thinking of the day, which, we are told, saw in surprise landings on open beaches the correct tactical approach to the problem. The emphasis here is on surprise, using the last hour of darkness to creep up on the enemy before he is fully awake. On lightly-defended beaches such as Pourville this was the proper technique, but Dieppe was not an open beach but a very heavily-defended position, with the defences favoured both by nature and art. To hope for surprise here was optimistic, but it might have come off *if the timing had been right.* But the timing was not right, and upwards of 2,000 men were committed to a frontal assault on a fortress manned by an alert and wide-awake enemy.

Certainly the planners were working on an incorrect assessment of the enemy strength. There were many things they did not know, but what they did know should have told them that a heavy bombardment or the absolute maximum of surprise was vital. Without one of the other how could they hope for any success?

Reference to the military thinking of the day does not help us on this point, which is one of the least explicable features of 'Jubilee', unless one faces up to the thought that this was indeed a sacrifice landing, which would not properly serve its purpose unless the going was really tough.

It should be made clear that Canadian officers had nothing to do with the preparation of the outline plan, which was the work of C.O.H.Q. and General Montgomery, as representative of Home Forces Command. The first the Canadians knew of the impending operation was on 30th April, when Montgomery informed General McNaughton, G.O.C.-in-C. Canadian 1st Army, that a raid on Dieppe was planned and that it had been decided to employ Canadian

153

troops from South-Eastern Command. McNaughton was delighted that at last his men were to get the action they craved, and delegated responsibility for the operation to General Crerar, G.O.C. 1st Canadian Corps, who nominated the 2nd Canadian Division, commanded by General Roberts, for the task. Roberts was instructed to start work on the detailed planning in conjunction with General Montgomery and C.O.H.Q. On 5th May a directive was issued by the Commander-in-Chief, Home Forces, which sought to clarify the relationship between Home Forces and the Chief of Combined Operations in connection with raids. This provided that once the C-in-C. Home Forces had decided from which command the troops for a raid were to be drawn, he would delegate responsibility for the operation to the G.O.C.-in-C. that command. The latter could retain the responsibility himself or delegate it to an officer not below the rank of divisional commander. This officer and his staff would then participate in the preparation of an outline plan in conjunction with the planning staffs of Home Forces and C.O.H.Q. When the outline plan was approved by the Chiefs of Staff, force commanders would be appointed and these officers would be responsible for the detailed plan. In this instance, Montgomery did not delegate the responsibility but kept it in his own hands. The Canadians were given a ready-made plan, instructed to study it and report back, or, in Army parlance, make an 'appreciation' of it.

The plan, as submitted to General Roberts and his staff, called for a frontal attack on Dieppe preceded by a heavy bomber assault during the night. It was approved and the approval signed by the 2nd Division's G.S.O. 1, Lt.-Col. (later Brigadier C. C. Mann, who, after discussing the pros and cons of a frontal attack, with particular emphasis on the use of tanks, came to the conclusion that the pros outweighed the cons. General McNaughton, who had been empowered by his Government to commit Canadian troops to any operation of which he himself approved, also accepted the proposed arrangements. Detailed planning by the combined British and Canadian staffs was already in progress.

At this stage General McNaughton could, if he chose, have rejected the outline plan, but there seemed no good reason for so doing. Indeed, at that time no Canadian officer would have been willing to reject any plan which promised action. With all ranks spoiling for a fight, to do so might have meant removal from his command and would certainly have earned him the anger and contempt of his officers and men.

At a meeting of C.O.H.Q. on 5th June, presided over by General Montgomery, the decision was taken to drop the bombardment. Although, as we have said, this seemed to be unanimous, unanimity was not reached without much argument. Both the Naval and Air Force representatives, Hughes-Hallett and Leigh-Mallory, thought that without bombardment the frontal attack was too hazardous, and the plan should either be altered or abandoned altogether. But the Army officers, and especially the Canadians, would not hear of it. They stated in no uncertain terms that this was an Army matter and that the sailors and airmen should confine themselves to their own provinces.

So the fateful decision was made and the first nail hammered into 'Jubilee's' coffin.

Roberts, at least, seemed worried at the lack of fire-power and asked Mountbatten to apply to the Admiralty for a battleship, only to be told that any such request was certain to be refused.

The ensuing weeks saw the operation mounted, cancelled and revived. During this period there occurred some changes in the chain of command, consequent upon Montgomery's departure to Egypt to take over the Eighth Army. McNaughton had himself appointed as responsible officer for operations carried out by troops under his command, as from 24th July, and on 27th July he formally delegated responsibility to General Crerar, in accordance with the Home Forces directive of 5th May. Crerar formally appointed Roberts as force commander for the operation, now known as 'Jubilee'.

The Canadians now had full military control of the plan, subject only to Mountbatten. It was theirs to do what they liked with, and much criticism has recently been directed at the three senior Canadian officers, in particular Roberts, for not having altered or even cancelled the whole affair. This seems most unfair to Roberts, who had inherited a plan already accepted by his superior officers. To go back on it now, when they had full military responsibility, would be tantamount to sabotage, and would certainly have spelt finis to the career of whoever dared to do so. If they did not like the plan, or any part of it, the time to have said so was after 5th June, when the bombardment was dispensed with, but, misled as to the enemy strength, confident that a surprise landing could be effected, urged on by Home Forces Command and C.O.H.Q., and conscious of the urgent political desire for a diversion in the west, the Canadians stifled their doubts – if, indeed, they ever had any doubts.

On 11th August Crerar reported to McNaughton that he was satisfied with the arrangements and was of the opinion that 'given an even break in luck ... the operation should prove successful.'

On the 14th August McNaughton went over the plans Crerar and Roberts, and he too expressed satisfaction with everything and formally sanctioned the participation of Canadian troops in the raid. On 17th August the question of bombing was reviewed once again by Mountbatten and the force commanders. General Roberts was still convinced that bomb debris in the narrow streets would prevent the tanks from getting through, and the decision in this regard was maintained. Shortly before this meeting, Roberts had briefed his senior staff officers on the revived operation. The news that Dieppe was again the target and that there would be no bombardment was received with something akin to consternation, and much of the previous enthusiasm for action vanished. We have already indicated that the troops were considerably disquieted when told they were once again en route to Dieppe. Survivors speak of a strange tension which gripped the whole Division on the voyage – a tension which went beyond what might have been expected of men about to undergo their baptism of fire. Probably never before had a force so full of forebodings set off to battle, and how soon were their worst fears to be realized.

While it may have been impossible, for a variety of reasons, for the Canadians to have withdrawn from the operation, even if they had wanted to, they could, with profit, have made some alterations in the plan, without incurring displeasure or reprisals from above. For example, if they had wished to retain the bombardment, why not have struck out the attempt on the airfield and the seizure of the barges? In the former instance, any delay in getting the tanks through the streets would not have mattered when they had not to support the attack on the airfield. A few bulldozers would have been useful for clearance purposes. Secondly, to get the barges out of the harbour, an electrically-operated dock bridge had to be lifted and if the power-house had been damaged by bombs this could not be done. Sinking the vessels in the harbour would have solved that problem and given the enemy much more trouble than removing them altogether. Both these minor objectives were only of propaganda value, and if dispensed with, the principal objection to the bombing was gone. These matters seem so obvious that one wonders why something of the sort was not arranged. Better an inaccurate bombardment than none at all, if only for the confusion and demoralizing effect on the garrison. We were to see this exemplified two years later on D-Day, when a colossal bombardment from sea and air was 75 per cent unsuccessful in destroying enemy positions, but had a tremendously demoralizing effect on the troops manning them. In one place a whole battalion ran away.

But there was to be no aerial bombardment. Bomber Command wanted no part of the operation, which was likely to interfere with their pre-arranged programme of attacks on Germany. They said, quite rightly, that accuracy could not be guaranteed, and if there was a cloud condition on the night, the heavy bombers might not find Dieppe at all. Roberts, as force commander, could have insisted on a bombardment, but in face of expert opinion as to the probable results, decided to dispense with it and pin his hopes on surprise.

It seems he was concerned at the time lag in the main landings, but got no help here from the Navy, who said they could not get the troops to the beach any earlier.

The operation now took on a suicidal appearance, and if conditions generally had been normal, it would in all likelihood have been scrapped. But conditions were far from normal – somehow, somewhere, this way or that, an assault on the enemy coast had to be made. This was Roberts's dilemma. If he rejected the plan against the wishes and pressure from above, he would almost certainly have been removed from his post and the operation mounted just the same under another force commander. On the other hand, if he accepted, there was always the faint hope that good luck might see them through. The fundamental error would seem to be the adherence to a set plan, which should have been modified to suit altered conditions. In other words, have a bombardment and reduce the objectives, or, with no bombardment, devise some other method of assaulting the main beaches.

In the upshot, of course, Roberts got the blame, although both McNaughton and Crerar had quite as much a part in the affair. But such is harsh military custom – a general who loses a battle, no matter how, is never given a second chance. Roberts finished out the war in command of a reinforcement establishment, and with his departure from the active scene went the only senior Army officer in Britain who had experience of amphibious assaults under actual battle conditions. Such are the ways of governments.

General Roberts has been vilified by many people uninformed of the full facts behind the Dieppe operation, but, far from being an object of vilification, he is deserving of sympathy, along with all those other commanders in history who failed in an impossible task.

He must have realized that the affair bore the stamp of a sacrifice attack and that there was nothing in it for him except personal disaster. Yet he played the part of a man and a soldier in undertaking it, knowing that in doing so he ran the risk of odium for ever after.

There is an ironic twist to all this in the thought that while on a day in early June, the planners were signing the death-warrant of hundreds of Canadian soldiers, they were at the same time giving a new lease of life to hundreds of French men, women and children, who otherwise would have perished in the shambles of Dieppe.

In the final count Canadian casualties alone totalled 3,400, out of a force of 5,000 engaged. Of this number over 900 were dead, and most of the rest prisoners, many of them wounded. The Commandos lost about 270, in killed, wounded and prisoners, chiefly at Berneval and in the naval battle. The Royal Navy had 550 casualties and the R.A.F. 153, many of the latter being prisoners.

The 2nd Canadian Division was practically wiped out – not since the blood-bath of the Somme in 1916 had a formation suffered such losses. For weeks afterwards bodies of drowned soldiers and sailors were washed up all along the French coast.

The Official Canadian History has calculated that almost 1,000 men did not land. This includes the bulk of No. 3 Commando, part of the Royal Marine Commando, half the Tank Regiment and various groups from different units whose landing-craft had broken down on the voyage or could not get in close enough to the beaches to put their men ashore. It follows, therefore, that more than three-quarters of the force actually landed became casualties, either killed, wounded or prisoners. Material losses were one destroyer, H.H.S. *Berkeley*, and thirty-three landing-craft of various types, twenty-eight Churchill tanks and one American 32-tonner, a few scout cars, some of which went down with the sunken tank landing-craft, and a large quantity of stores and equipment of all sorts. R.A.F. losses were heavy, no less than 108 aircraft being shot down, including 98 fighters.

The enemy losses totalled 591, killed, wounded and prisoners; of the last-named very few were brought back, some being killed by their own guns and others escaping when the ships they were in were sunk. German material losses were less than was thought. In addition to the six-gun battery destroyed at Quiberville, two beach-defence guns at Pourville were wrecked, and many machine-gun nests on the West Hill and elsewhere put out of action. Some of the anti-aircraft batteries were silent during the latter part of the battle, and two of the anti-tank weapons sited at the Casino were blown up. The tobacco factory was set on fire and burnt out. This building, a prominent landmark on the sea front, was thought to contain explosives, but this seems unlikely as there are no reports of any explosion having occurred during the burning. It was also reported that the gasworks had been destroyed, but this was incorrect. It had been damaged by shelling or bombing, but was working again two days later. It had certainly been an objective of the troops landing at Puys, but as it was a long way back from the sea front it seems unlikely that any party penetrated so far inland. It was also reported that the radar station on the cliffs to the west of Dieppe had been destroyed. This again was incorrect. Many of the buildings on the sea front in the occupation of the enemy were destroyed or damaged by shell-fire. The German naval losses were: one

of the submarine-chasers escorting the convoy from Boulogne, sunk with all hands, one badly damaged, and the
tanker *Franz*, which was sunk at Berneval by M.L.346. The
Luftwaffe lost forty-eight aircraft, although it was claimed
at the time that many more had been shot down.

On balance, then, a decided victory for the Germans, who
had repelled what they considered an invasion attempt at
comparatively small cost.

Dieppe taught the Germans that they could stop an invasion attempt on the beaches. What did it teach the
British?

Combined Operations H.Q. opened their list of 'Lessons
Learned' with the statement: 'Many lessons were learnt at
Dieppe, *not all of them new.*' The lesson of greatest importance was the need for overwhelming fire support, including
close support, during the initial stages of an attack. Any veteran of the 1914–18 war could have told them that. Next
was the need, in any future amphibious assault, of a properly
organized and trained permanent naval force to handle the
various types of landing-ship and assault craft. This was a
procedure which Captain Hughes-Hallett, R.N., had been ad-
vocating for a long time, but his was a voice crying in the
wilderness until Dieppe. The third most important lesson
was the need for specially equipped and organized headquarters ships, manned by permanent trained crews representing all three Services. Only thus could force commanders hope to control a battle and carry out a flexible
plan. In addition, many valuable technical lessons were
learnt – in the use of smoke (which was excellent at Dieppe;
the value of cannon-fighter attacks as diversions, but not as a
substitute for bombardment; the shortcomings of the equipment available, especially in the field of close support; the
inadvisability of landing beach signal-parties and tanks until
the beaches were under control; the need of some form of
armoured vehicle to give shelter to demolition parties, and
the necessity that all future assaults on heavily-defended
areas should be planned to develop around the flanks rather
than frontally. Finally, the idea of securing bridge-heads by
means of surprise landings over open beaches was abandoned for good, and with it went the previously held view
that the seizure of a port was a vital requirement of invasion.

Writing of Dieppe, Sir Winston Churchill said, 'Looking back, the casualties of this memorable action may seem out of proportion to the results. It would be wrong to judge the episode solely by such a standard. Dieppe occupies a place of its own in the story of war, and the grim casualty figures must not class it a failure. It was a costly but not unfruitful reconnaissance in force. Tactically it was a mine of experience. It shed revealing light on many shortcomings in our outlook. It taught us to build in good time various types of craft and appliances for later use. We learnt again the value of powerful support by heavy guns in an opposed landing, and our bombardment technique, both marine and aerial, was thereafter improved ... My general impression of "Jubilee" is that the results fully justified the heavy cost. The large-scale air-battle alone justified the raid.'

After the Normandy landings in June 1944, General Crerar, commanding the 1st Canadian Army, said, 'I think it is most important, at this time, that all of you should realize what a vital part the gallant and hazardous operation of the raid in force on Dieppe has played in the conception, planning and execution of the vast "Overlord" operation. Until the evidence of Dieppe proved otherwise, it had been the opinion in highest command and staff circles in this country that an assault against a heavily-defended coast could be carried out on the basis of securing tactical surprise, and without dependence on overwhelming fire support in the critical phases of closing the beaches and overrunning the beach defences. If tactical surprise was to be the basis of the plan, the bombardment prior to imminent touch-down obviously requires to be ruled out. Dependence on tactical surprise also implies an approach under cover of darkness and landing at first light.

'... Although at the time the heavy cost to Canada and the non-success of the Dieppe operation seemed hard to bear, I believe that when this war is examined in proper perspective, it will be seen that the sobering influence of this operation ... was a Canadian contribution of the greatest significance to final victory.'

And what were the opinions of those men whose contribution to final victory was to spend two years in a German prisoner-of-war camp, counting themselves lucky that they were not numbered among their dead comrades, whose bodies littered the Dieppe beaches? The following extract from a letter written by a survivor of Blue Beach about sums up those opinions:

'After boarding the ship we were told we were going to Dieppe, and right then I and the rest of the boys knew we had lost our main weapon, the element of surprise. Which proved to be true, because when fourteen miles off the coast of France the whole Channel was lit up like daylight from the Germans. Right then in my heart I knew we were in for one hell of a time, and the chance of success had been replaced by a fight for survival. Every man knew his job, and after months of training was eager to get a crack at the enemy. I know that this was not only in my heart but in the hearts of every Canadian soldier on board those ships. We wanted to give a damn good show, to the world, to Canada and to the Germans. We were not afraid despite the odds, and we would do our jobs whatever we ran into when we landed. You can imagine our feelings when we were spotted and knew we were sitting ducks at the mercy of God and the Germans. We landed in terrific fire, in broad daylight with no smoke-cover. Everything seemed to go wrong – confusion and uncertainty reigned – we had lost our knock-out punch. I shall always remember, after the surrender, the faces of the survivors, officers and men, sitting on the beach among our dead, crying. We felt robbed – robbed of the chance to fight and show what we could do. We had the right kind of men and the equipment to put up one hell of a fight, but the whole affair was a failure because we were not given the chance to land as an organized unit, but as a confused, bewildered bunch of men seeking shelter and defending our lives as best we could. Such it was, on the beach, where the Royal Regiment landed – a massacre, a bloody mess.'

Here we have two different approaches to the matter. The statesman and the general point to lessons learnt as justification for the losses. The private soldier, seeing only the blood and death of the beaches, condemns the blunder which places himself and his comrades in an impossible position. He does not worry or care about the deeper motives of the expedition. He has a job to do and is eager to do it. He puts his trust in his leaders and is let down. To him the whole thing appears stupid and senseless.

Of course, he is completely right in his summing-up – but are the others equally correct in theirs? Did 'Jubilee' justify itself in the long run? A close analysis of the claims made for it may cause one to think it did not.

For a start, Winston Churchill was wrong in stating that the air-battle alone justified the raid. It did nothing of the sort. His assertion is probably based on the erroneous R.A.F. claim to have destroyed ninety-one German aircraft and damaged twice that number. In fact, captured records show that German losses were forty-eight destroyed and twenty-four damaged. Against R.A.F. losses of 106 shot down, this could only be hailed as a Pyrrhic victory – not at all the crippling blow which the R.A.F. hoped to deal the Luftwaffe.

It will have been noted that these eminent people, in their speeches and writings, refer only to the military side of the operation, saying nothing about the political implications, although there can be no doubt that political motives weighed heavier than military demands in mounting the operation.

From the political angle it achieved very little. While it stilled the communist-inspired clamour in Britain for a second front, it failed to satisfy Stalin, who continued to demand early action in France. Not unnaturally, the Russians took the view that if the British could take such losses for a mere raid, they must be strong enough to undertake a more ambitious project. As far as affording military relief to the Russians by causing the withdrawal of troops from the east, 'Jubilee' was a failure. Such German redeployments as were made had no effect on the Russian front.

From the military aspect, it is claimed that much benefit derived from 'Jubilee', the more so because of the extent of the failure.

An examination of the lessons learnt, as announced by C.O.H.Q., who admitted, that not all were new, gives one food for thought. Firstly, it is said that the outcome of the Dieppe raid caused the abandonment of the idea of seizing a port and of the theory of achieving tactical surprise in a landing. The first is correct, but we do not think the second is wholly true. The Army chiefs were not as obsessed with this idea as General Crerar's speech would seem to indicate. It will be remembered that the first Dieppe plan included a heavy preliminary bombardment, which was dropped, not because of an obsession with the theory of surprise, but because various technical reasons were advanced against it. With no bombardment, and with an operation as inevitable as 'Jubilee', there was nothing left but surprise.

The clear implication of Crerar's statement is that if there had been no 'Jubilee' there would have been no bombardment on D-Day, which is arrant nonsense. Would any sane commander have founded an operation of the magnitude of D-Day on the chancy basis of securing surprise. with all its implications of split-second timing and precision. We do not think so.

It is certain that as the German defences grew and sprouted along the beaches, the planners would realize that the only guarantee of success lay in employing the full weight of aerial and naval bombardment – which, of course, is exactly what they did on D-Day. Not because Dieppe taught them anything, but because it was the only way of breaching the enemy defences. The Combined Operations Report on Dieppe states quite clearly that as the German defences increased, so the chance of obtaining tactical surprise decreased. This refutes the claim that we had to go to Dieppe to 'learn again the value of powerful naval guns in an opposed landing'.

As for 'various types of craft and appliances', surely most of these would have been developed as the problem of overcoming the German coastal defences was studied and appraised.

The need for close support at the moment of touch-down was well understood. Everybody knew the most dangerous time for the attackers in an opposed landing was while they were disembarking and forming up into proper order. At Dieppe several special craft were used to come in to the beach to give covering fire. Being lightly armoured and equipped only with machine-guns and smoke-mortars, they proved largely ineffective against the heavy enemy fire. From this experience evolved the landing-craft gun, a shallow-draught vessel fitted with an artillery piece, which could be operated close inshore. Here again this and the rocket ships would surely have come into existence as the concrete emplacements appeared on the French beaches.

Another 'lesson' claimed was the need of a properly equipped H.Q. ship, but this was not new, as just such a vessel was in course of preparation (H.M.S. *Bulolo*), although not ready to participate in the raid. Where communications were concerned, the big lesson was the inadvisability of landing beach signal-parties until the beach was under control. This should have been obvious, as the German sniper technique of picking off men with special equipment was well known.

About the only really new appliance originating from Dieppe was the Armoured Vehicle Royal Engineers A.V.R.E., a tracked vehicle designed to give protection to demolition parties while engaged in their tasks. We have seen how, without such shelter, the sappers at Dieppe were foiled in their attempts to breach the anti-tank obstacles on the Promenade.

Of course, something was learnt about the merits or demerits of the equipment taken ashore, but it seems the most significant contribution made by 'Jubilee' was the decision to abandon any attempt to seize a port, a decision which led to the development of the Mulberry Harbour. History attributes this decision to Captain Hughes-Hallet and/or Winston Churchill, but whoever was responsible, it was indeed revolutionary thinking, beside which all else was mere routine.

When the armies of the west appeared off the beaches on D-Day, they brought with them a great variety of weapons – amphibious tanks (some of which proved not so amphibious, flame-throwing tanks, flail tanks for beating up minefields, close-support craft with banks of rocket-throwers, other devices of destruction. Were all these the results of experience at Dieppe? Were they not the offspring of the cumulative experience of many amphibious attacks – from North Africa, Sicily, Italy and the many American assaults in the Far East?

That eminent historian, Colonel Stacey, in his magnificent and monumental work on the history of the Canadian Army during 1939–45, says,* 'It is doubtful whether any other operation had as much influence as Dieppe upon the Normandy planning. A full analysis of that influence would require a chapter to itself . . .'

* *Six Years of War*, page 403.

Unfortunately, he does not give us that chapter, but simply compares the Dieppe and Normandy assault plans, with reference to the Dieppe lessons, which we have already enumerated.

He admits that while some new lessons were learnt at Dieppe, it was not necessary to attack the port to learn them. His comparison of the bombardment techniques of the two landings (four destroyers at Dieppe against five battleships and nineteen cruisers on D-Day) does not take into account the comparative size and importance of the two operations. On the whole, his pronouncements on 'Jubilee's' influence on later operations are not really convincing. He is on somewhat safer ground in his opinion of 'Jubilee's' effect on Allied military thinking, pointing to the over-optimistic view held by American officers on the problem of invasion, and stating that the history of the Dieppe planning indicated that British officers also underrated the difficulties.

On the subject of tactical surprise, Colonel Stacey quotes General Crerar's speech, which we have mentioned above, and seeks to substantiate the general's view by stating that the planning of two major assaults intended to seize permanent bridge-heads in France* – one in the Le Havre area and the other on the Cherbourg peninsula – laid great emphasis on the importance of surprise and none at all upon naval or air bombardment. Without detailed knowledge of the exact points of attack, and as neither venture ever got beyond the planning stage, it is not possible to assess the value of Colonel Stacey's support for Crerar's statements. For all we know, the proposed landings might have been intended for lightly-defended beaches such as Pourville, and achieving surprise the correct way to assault them. It must be remembered that at this time, the autumn of 1942, German defences were sketchy along the whole coast, except in the vicinity of seaports.

In any event, we simply do not believe that the Army commanders thought the only way of assaulting strongly-held beaches frontally was by surprise. At Dieppe this decision was forced upon them by pressure of outside events, and was not a fair sample of their ideas on the tactics of major assaults. Certainly never again would they commit such a blunder – but tactical surprise was still a useful

* 'Sledgehammer' and 'Wetbob'.

weapon under certain circumstances, as was to be proved a year later at Salerno.

One of the unexpected dividends claimed for 'Jubilee' was its effect on German military thinking, but this must not be over-estimated. As far back as March 1942, Hitler had signed a directive which, *inter alia*, called for the immediate development of the defence system on the western coast, with special attention to seaports. On 11th June Washington and London issued communiqués on the conference with Molotov, who had come to seek an early opening of the second front. These communiques stated that 'full understanding had been reached with regard to the urgent tasks of creating a second front in Europe in 1942'. We have referred to this rather irresponsible statement elsewhere, but its effect on the Germans was to cause them to take immediate special measures. Not only were the digging and pouring of concrete stepped up, but important reinforcements of crack troops were moved from Germany into France. On 2nd August, Hitler laid down his requirements for the West Wall – 'a solid line with unbroken fire must be insisted on at all costs' – and on 13th August the result of a further conference with his chiefs may be summed up thus: 'The Führer has decided to build an impregnable fortress along the Atlantic and Channel coasts.'

Always had Hitler believed that an invasion could and must be stopped on the beaches. The 'Jubilee' operation served to confirm this theory, but did not affect in any way the long-term programme of fortification. Work on the West Wall continued as planned, but at an accelerated pace, due to persistent reports from German agents of troop concentrations in southern England.

As we have said, the Germans' eyes were fixed on the French coast, but not particularly as a result of the Dieppe landings.

In the preceding pages we have examined the oft-repeated claim that the Dieppe raid had a profound effect on the planning of the Normandy landings, and have suggested that this effect has been considerably exaggerated. We have shown that some of the beneficial results claimed did not arise from the action, and others would have come about anyway, in the natural order of things.

What, then, was the value of the operation to the future conduct of the war? We venture to say, very little. Every battle contributes something to the next one, but 'Jubilee's' contribution would appear to have been over-rated. As the first step in a process of evolution, it had its importance, and, no doubt owing to its fiery start, the development of that process was quickened, but to point to all the might and majesty of D-Day and declare that all this originated on the beaches of Dieppe is to over-emphasize the influence of what was after all a disastrous experiment, and to overlook the credit due to the many later sea-borne attacks undertaken by the Allies.

Even the alleged sobering influence of 'Jubilee' upon the Allied commanders was not really necessary. So far as the British were concerned, Winston Churchill, with the bitter memory of Dunkirk still fresh in his mind, was unlikely to be stampeded into any rash continental adventures. He had already handed his 'no invasion' pill to the Americans, who had stomached it unwillingly and with distaste, and long before Dieppe had accepted in principle the British strategy of attacking the enemy at widely-separated points on his extended perimeter, as against their own strategy of a head-on frontal attack, depending on weight to smash their way through and accepting the probability of severe losses to gain a quick and decisive success.

Once the North-African assault plan was adopted, the invasion of Western Europe was automatically put back for at least a couple of years. Any American hope of invasion in 1943 vanished because the armies necessary for such an undertaking just did not exist.

Having come thus far, it is only fair to relate that an article on Dieppe, recently published in a Canadian newspaper, quotes the views of many of the senior Canadian officers who took part in the raid, and one and all they are in agreement that it was worth while – for the reasons which we have already mentioned.

Perhaps one could hardly expect them to say otherwise in their public utterances, which seem part and parcel of the smoke-screen of high-sounding words which had always clouded the operation – a screen which tends to dissipate under the searching light of close analysis. Naturally everybody concerned with the affair would endeavour to salvage what comfort they could from the ashes of defeat, but it is going a bit too far to claim almost miraculous results and influences from what was, after all, but a minor action when seen against the over-all picture of the war.

We have shown the reverse side of the medal, and it is up to the thoughtful reader to decide for himself where lies the truth. But whatever his judgment, one thing brooks no denial – the guinea-pigs of Dieppe, sacrificed to the God of War, can rightly claim 'for your tomorrow we gave our today'.

One final point remains to be cleared up. Many people, unaware of the full details, expressed disappointment with the performance of the Canadians at Dieppe, indicating the large number of prisoners taken as justification for their view. It is true that the German 81st Corps H.Q. issued a report in which the Canadians were compared unfavourably with the Commandos. This report stated that 'the 2nd Division were loaded on to transports and shipped into action without the soldiers being told either the objective or the mission. The troops on the whole fought badly and surrendered afterwards in swarms.' As we know, this is entirely false, and is directly contradicted and repudiated by the reports of the German 15th Army H.Q. and the 302nd Division, which commended as follows:

'The large number of prisoners might leave the impression that the fighting value of the English and Canadian units employed should not be too highly estimated. This is not the case. The enemy, almost entirely Canadian soldiers, fought – so far as he was able to fight at all – well and bravely, and the chief reasons for the large number of prisoners and casualties are probably:

1. Lack of artillery support.
2. Underestimation of the defences which placed the enemy in a hopeless position immediately he came ashore.
3. The effect of our defensive weapons was superior to that of the weapons employed by the attacker.
4. The craft provided for re-embarkation were almost all hit and sunk.

'At Dieppe, his tank crews did not lack spirit, but could not penetrate the anti-tank walls barring the way into the town.

'At Puys, the efforts made by the enemy, in spite of heavy German machine-gun fire, to surmount the wire obstacles studded with booby traps on the first beach terrace are signs of a good offensive spirit. The large number of prisoners here was the result of the hopelessness of the situation for the men who had landed, caught under heavy German machine-gun and mortar fire on a beach which offered no cover.

'At Pourville, the enemy, immediately after landing, pushed forward into the interior without worrying about flank protection.

'The operations against the coastal batteries were conducted by the Commandos with great dash and skill. With the aid of technical devices of all sorts they succeeded in clambering up the steep cliffs at points which had seemed inaccessible.'

This then is the viewpoint of the German 302nd Division, the formation in direct contact with the attackers. Who should know better than they?

It is now generally admitted that Dieppe was no action for troops inexperienced in battle, but even had battle-seasoned units been employed, it is questionable whether they could have done any better under the double handicap of lack of surprise and artillery support, and in view of the appalling conditions existing on the beaches.

The Official Canadian History tells us that the effect throughout the Canadian Army was tremendous. In spite of what was undoubted defeat, the action produced a new sense of pride in the Army. Gone was the disappointment and frustration of nearly three years, to be replaced by a great uplift in morale. The young men of Canada had proved they could fight as well as their fathers had done in 1914–18, but their enthusiasm and eagerness for the fray were tempered by the knowledge that only by the most rigorous training and discipline could they fit themselves for the tough task that lay ahead.

On 1st September, 1944, the 2nd Canadian Division returned to Dieppe. The port had been given up by the Germans without a fight, and those few who remained of the 1942 raid walked over the ground they had once fought for. They found the graves of their comrades well cared for by the local people, and on 3rd September the whole division staged a victory march-past. At last, the wheel had come full circle.

Epilogue

FIRST publication of this book in July 1963 caused a remarkable revival of interest in this always somewhat mysterious operation, and again raised the question – did the Germans have advance knowledge of the Raid? I have stated quite definitely that they did not, but in spite of this, various newspaper articles and letters have appeared seeking to prove that the contrary was the case. Under the circumstances I consider it advisable to collect together in one chapter all the evidence both for, and against, the theory. Much of that upon which I base my conclusions has already appeared in preceding pages, but some repetition is unavoidable if a clear and compact picture is to be presented.

The evidence brought forward in support of the theory of foreknowledge comprises extracts from directives issued by Hitler during the summer of 1942, concerning the movement of troops into France and the fortifying of the Channel coast.

It has been suggested that these directives prove that Hitler knew of the intention to attack Dieppe, but a careful study of them shows that they deal with the overall development of the defences of the West Wall, work on which was greatly accelerated in the summer of 1942, as a direct result of German victories in Russia, which led Hitler to believe that the British must launch an attack in the west, if Russia was to be kept in the war. Added conviction came with the news of top-level meetings between the Allied leaders and final proof was supplied by reports of the assemblages of small craft in various South of England ports.

Hitler warned that the assault could come anywhere on the coast from Brittany to the southern part of the Netherlands, but was paricularly nervous about the area between Le Havre and Calais, which is so convenient to England. The stream of directives which flowed from his H.Q.

frequently made mention of Dieppe as a likely target, but not any more so than half a dozen other points.

There is nothing on record to show especial preoccupation with the defence of Dieppe.

With the Hitler directives now seen in their proper perspective what other evidence has been adduced in favour of forewarning?

On 2nd October, 1963, the *Evening Standard* published an interview with Luftwaffe General Ulrich Kessler, who was Fliegerfuhrer, Atlantik at the time of the Raid and who stated that because the Germans had broken the British Naval Code, they became aware of the intention to attack Dieppe. At the conclusion of this interview the *Evening Standard* refers to a previously published article by a young English historian in which he made the same claim but winds up by asking 'Who told the Germans it was going to be Dieppe? Who has it on his conscience?' If his previous article was authentic, who else but Kessler?

In my correspondence with German officers who were involved in the Dieppe action I noticed a certain forgetfulness about some quite important details and what I could only describe as hindsight about others. However, I think the final authority on the question must be Captain Stephen Roskill, R.N., the official Naval Historian, who states in his magnificent work *The War at Sea* that the Enemy Wireless Intelligence Service made no reports on the expedition. Captain Roskill is confident that in spite of a partial breaking of the Naval Code, the Germans learnt nothing useful from our cyphered messages in so far as the Dieppe operation was concerned. He further points out that the German Abewehr (Secret Servise) H.Q. in Paris repeated that some of their agents had any indication that Dieppe was about to be attacked. (See his letter in *Daily Telegraph* of 4-11-63.)

A final fantastic piece of evidence was produced by the *Daily Sketch* on 4th October, 1963, when they published an article on Dieppe with a photograph of an advertisement for soap flakes which appeared in the British Press on 13th August, 1942. The picture shows a woman pruning a rose bush, using, not secateurs, but powerful looking wire-cutters, the heading reading, in large print, 'Beach Coat from Dieppe' while the small print refers to women buying such articles in Dieppe in pre-war days and suggests they should be washed in this particular brand of flakes. Needless to say, this caused no end of a flap in security circles in Britain, but investigation showed it to be entirely innocent. This could have been read by German agents in neutral countries and interpreted as a coded warning. Something similar occurred just before D-Day in June 1944, when the *Daily Telegraph* crossword contained, as answers to various clues, the code name of the operation, Overlord, and of the invasion beaches, Juno, Sword, Omaha, etc. Again, a fantastic co-incidence. However, the answer to the Dieppe problem lies in German records dealing directly with the battle and in a study of the situation at Dieppe on the night of 18th/19th August, 1942.

The most important German document in Von Runstedt's Battle Report issued from OB West on 3rd September, 1942. This report, document 24353/10 is entitled 'Gefechtsbericht uber Feindlandugen bei und beiderseits Dieppe am 19-8-42', and is a comprehensive analysis of events both before and during the actual operations against Dieppe. It indicates that from the middle of June 1942, increasing numbers of reports were received by OB West from Luftflotte 3 and agents, reporting on the basis of visual and photographic observations, about an assemblage of numerous small amphibious craft along the south coast of England. OB West took all precautionary measures to be prepared for some kind of enemy action, including having the troops standing to their guns on certain nights thought favourable for an assault. However there was no reported change in the overall enemy situation until 0450 hours on 19th August. Even the early morning reconnaissance report of Luftflotte 3 mentioned nothing unusual.

At 2100 hours on 18th August, a German Coastal convoy left Boulogne for Dieppe, sailing west, while another convoy from Le Harve was creeping along the coast and due to reach Dieppe about 0430 hours.

At 0450 hours the westbound convoy was attacked by surface craft off Dieppe. According to the initial evaluation of Mar. Gruppen Kdo, West (Naval Group Command West), this action was one of the usual attacks on coastal shipping. It caused no special alarm ashore, but some troops in the Puys area went to their posts.

Up to the beginning of operations on the morning of 19th August the German Wireless Intelligence covering England failed to notice anything unusual and Luftwaffe Intelligence reported that nothing out of the ordinary occurred which would indicate any immediate landing attempts.

This document makes it clear that nobody within Von Runstedt's area of command had any real foreknowledge of British intentions and this is fully confirmed by the overall picture of events at Dieppe on the night of 18th/19th August.

A brief summary of the situation there is as followed:

The lighthouses at Dieppe Harbour and Cap D'Ailly were flashing to guide in the two convoys which certainly would not have been allowed to sail into the area of an expected assault.

The collision between No. 3 Commando Group and the German Convoy caused me particular alarm ashore, although radar specialist troops at Puys manned their station there.

During the previous weeks, at danger periods, German troops stood by their guns all night, but on the night of 18th/19th August everything was normal and troops not on duty undressed and went to bed. This is confirmed by the Guard Book of the German Battery at Varengeville, captured by No. 4 Commando, which shows that only routine watches were kept. As already mentioned, OB West had ordered the cancellation of the full alert as from the night of 18th August, but the Divisional Commander countermanded this order, but would appear to have been satisfied if some of the forward positions were manned with the soldiers sleeping beside their guns. This situation is borne out by reports from French sources which tells us that the air-raid shelters were full of German soldiers in various stages of undress during the early stages of the attack. Luftwaffe pilots were away on night leave and no serious air attacks developed until nearly five hours after touchdown when fighters and dive bombers appeared. Heavy bombers were not seen until after eleven o'clock. No surface craft were sighted at any time during the day.

There were no tanks in the area, the nearest being at Amiens, where a large formation was stationed ready to move to any threatened part of the coast. In the event, the leading units did not reach Dieppe until 1430 hours.

The German 302nd Division was short of transport and when the attack came had to make do with requisitioned buses and trucks to bring up their reserves.

At the seven points of assault, from Berneval to Varengeville, surprise was achieved on five beaches. At Berneval, the remnants of No. 3 Commando met no opposition until at least fifteen minutes after landing, while at Belleville Major Young's little party was undetected until they opened fire on the Battery. On the right flank, No. 4 Commando obtained complete surprise at both their landing points, as did the Canadians at Pourville. Only at Dieppe and Puys was there no surprise, faulty navigation, lack of close support and bad timing contributing to the disaster on these beaches.

A review of the Dieppe scene as it was in the early morning of 19th August presents a picture of normality which one would hardly associate with an army expectant of imminent assault. This is confirmed by the official C.O.H.Q. view of the affair, which reports that the state of readiness of the Germans was less than had been expected.

Finally let us take the opinions of the men who survived Puys and Dieppe whose briefing had indicated that only slight resistance would be encountered during the initial stages of the landings. Those going for Puys knew well in advance that there was to be no surprise, once the searchlights picked them out, but practically every man who came off Dieppe beach alive was convinced that the enemy had been forewarned.

The promised bombardment, to soften-up the defences, proved to be totally ineffective while the terrible reception that greeted their landing seemed proof enough that the enemy was ready and waiting, as we know he was, although not because of a tip-off.

One senior Canadian officer, who was on the beach from beginning to end told me that at no time during the day did he see any movement of supplies into the enemy forward positions, thus proving to his satisfaction that they were already stocked up for a day's shooting.

In fact, we know from German sources that every position had no less than four weeks' supplies of ammunition. Also the fortified houses and hotels fronting the beach could be entered and supplied from the rear out of sight of the beach. This same officer relates how, after the cancellation of the July operation, he walked into the open and deserted Ops. H.Q. at Cowes and picked up maps and orders from waste-paper baskets, as could anyone else. He just does not believe that of 5,000 men running loose on leave all over England, not one talked or mentioned Dieppe. Of course some did, but if German records are to be believed, nothing leaked out.

I should be reluctant to criticize any Dieppe veteran for his opinion, but there is an old Irish saying that the hurler on the ditch sees most of the game, which might be applicable and I would sum up the whole matter by saying that while the Germans feared an invasion attempt at that time, nobody knew when or where or how it would come.

Appendix 1

ORDER OF BATTLE

ROYAL NAVY

COMPOSITION OF FLEET

H.M.S. Destroyers, *Calpe, Fernie, Brocklesby, Garth, Albrighton, Berkeley, Bleasdale,* O.R.P. *Slazak*	
H.M. Gunboat *Locust*	1
H.M. Spool *Alresford*	1
Fighting French Chasseurs	7
Infantry Landing-Ships (L.S.I.)	9
Steam Gunboats (S.G.B.)	4
Motor Gunboats (M.G.B.)	12
Motor Launches (M.L.)	16
Tank Landing-Craft (L.C.T.)	24
Flak Ships (L.C.F.)	6
Support Landing-Craft (L.C.S.)	8
Motor Landing-Craft (L.C.M.)	7
Personnel Landing-Craft (L.C.P.)	74
Assault Landing-Craft (L.C.A.)	60
	237

TASKS L.S.I. and landing-craft. To put the troops ashore on the right beaches at the right time. Afterwards to get them safely back to England.

Other ships. To protect the landing-craft throughout the passages out and back.

ROYAL AIR FORCE

COMPOSITION OF FORCE

	Squadrons
Spitfires – Mark V	42
Spitfires – Mark VI	2
Spitfires – Mark IX	4
Hurricanes	6
Mustangs (Tac. R.)	4
Typhoons	2
Hurricanes (Fighter-Bomber)	2
Boston Bombers	3
Blenheim Bombers	2
	—
	67

UNITED STATES ARMY AIR FORCE

	Squadrons
Fighters	3
Fortress Bombers	4
	—
	7

TASKS To provide cover throughout the day.
To attack enemy coast defences and batteries.
To lay smoke-cover over East Headland during assault and withdrawal.
Tac. R. units to keep watch on enemy movements inland.
U.S.A.A.F. To attack enemy airfield at Abbeville.

In charge of proceedings – Air Marshal Leigh-Mallory, from No. 11 Group H.Q. at Uxbridge.
Air Liaison Officer afloat – Air Commodore Cole.

ARMY

H.Q. 2nd Canadian Division
2nd Canadian Div. Intelligence Section
2nd Canadian Div. F.S. Section
H.Q. 4th Canadian Inf. Brigade – Brigadier S. Lett
J. Sec. 2nd Canadian Div. Signals
Royal Regiment of Canada – Lt.-Col. Catto

Royal Hamilton Light Infantry – Lt.-Col. Labatt
Essex Scottish Regiment – Lt.-Col. Jasperson
H.Q. 6th Canadian Inf. Brigade – Brigadier Southam
L. Section 2nd Canadian Div. Signals
Fusiliers Mont Royal – Lt.-Col. Menard
Cameron Highlanders of Canada – Lt.-Col. Gostling
South Saskatchewan Regiment – Lt.-Col. Merritt
14th Canadian Army Tank Regiment – Lt.-Col. Andrews
7th Canadian Field Company
2nd Canadian Div. Signals

Detachments from:
8th Canadian Recce Regiment
R.H.C.
Calgary Highlanders
Toronto Scottish M.G.
R.C.A. units
R.C.A.S.C. units
R.C.A.M.C.
R.C.O.C.
Canadian Provost Corps
G.H.Q. Recce Regiment
Royal Canadian Engineers
Inter-Allied Commando
United States Army
No. 3 Commando – Lt.-Col. Durnford-Slater
No. 4 Commando – Lt.-Col. The Lord Lovat
Royal Marine Commando (under naval control until revert-
    ing) – Lt.-Col. Picton-Phillips

CHAIN OF COMMAND

Major-General Roberts – Military Force Commander

(1) Brigadier C. C. Mann – on H.Q. ship 2
(2) Brigadier Southam – 6th Can. Inf. Brigade
(3) Brigadier Sherwood Lett – 4th Can. Inf. Brigade
(4) Lt.-Col. Henderson – G.S.O.1. on H.Q. ship 1

Appendix 2

INTENTION AND PRINCIPAL OBJECTIVES

The 2nd Canadian Division will seize 'Jubilee' and vicinity Occupy the area until demolition and exploitation tasks are completed and then re-embark and return to England.

LEFT FLANK
Berneval – Yellow 1.
Belleville – Yellow 2.
No. 3 Commando. Lt.-Col. Durnford-Slater.
To destroy Goebbels battery near Berneval.

INNER LEFT
Puys – Blue.
Royal Regiment of Canada. Lt.-Col. Catto.
To destroy Rommel battery behind Puys and attack East Headland from rear.

CENTRE LEFT
Dieppe – Red.
Essex Scottish Regiment. Lt.-Col. Jasperson.

CENTRE RIGHT
Dieppe – White.
Royal Hamilton Light Infantry. Lt.-Col. Labbatt.
To support Red and White Beaches. 14th Canadian Army Tank Battalion (Calgary Regiment). Lt.-Col. Andrews.
In Reserve. Fusiliers Mont Royal. Lt.-Col. Menard.
In Reserve for special duty. Cutting out barges in harbour. Royal Marine 'A' Commando. Lt.-Col. Picton-Phillips.
To capture town and assist in capture of East and West Headlands. To hold harbour and remove barges.

INNER RIGHT   Pourville – Green.
South Saskatchewan Regt. Lt.-Col. Merritt.
Queen's Own Cameron Highlanders of Canada.
Lt.-Col. Gostling.
To capture fortified position Les Quatre Vents
Farm and attack from rear the West Headland.
Camerons to move through valley of River Scie
to capture aerodrome at St Aubyn and German
Divisional H.Q. at Arques-la-Bataille.

RIGHT FLANK   Varengeville-sur-Mer. Orange 1.
No. 4 Commando. Major D. Mills-Roberts.
To attack Hess battery from front.
Quiberville. East of River Saane. Orange 2.
No. 4 Commando. Lt.-Col. The Lord Lovat.
To attack Hess battery from rear.

Appendix 3

MATERIAL LOSSES

ROYAL NAVY	1 destroyer – H.M.S. *Berkeley*
	17 L.C.A.
	8 L.C.P.(L.)
	5 L.C.T.
	1 L.C.M.
	1 L.C.S.
	1 L.C.F.
	—
	34
MILITARY	28 Churchill tanks
	1 Sherman 32-tonner
	7 Scout cars
	2 5-cwt. cars
	1 Carrier
	3 Motor cycles
ROYAL AIR FORCE	88 Fighters
	10 Tactical Recce aircraft
	8 Bombers

DIEPPE RAID

Embarkation Strength   Casualties   Disembarkation Strength

2ND CANADIAN DIVISION

Unit	Number Embarked		Killed		Wounded		Prisoners		Number Returned	
	Offs.	ORs.	Offs.	ORs.	Offs.	ORs.	Offs.	ORs.	Offs.	ORs.
H.Q. & miscell.	42	48	5	—	7	7	4	11	33	37
Royal R.	26	528	10	215	2	31	14	250	2	63
R.H.L.I.	31	551	9	181	6	103	16	159	6	211
Essex Scottish	32	521	6	113	1	26	23	359	3	49
Mont R.	32	552	8	109	2	48	19	325	5	120
Camerons	32	471	5	63	9	94	9	158	18	250
South Sasks	25	498	3	78	7	159	9	80	13	340
Tank Reg.	32	385	2	11	—	4	15	142	15	232
Toronto Scottish	5	120	—	1	—	8	—	4	5	115
Black Watch	4	107	1	3	—	6	2	61	1	43
Calgary H'landers	1	21	—	—	—	—	—	—	1	21
R.C.A.	14	256	2	11	1	3	4	26	8	219
R.C.E.	7	309	2	24	3	33	1	124	4	161
R. Can. Signals	6	72	—	9	2	7	1	16	5	47
R.C.A.S.C.	1	37	—	1	—	6	1	3	—	33
R.C.A.M.C.	10	116	—	4	—	3	1	11	9	101
R.C.O.C.	1	14	—	2	—	2	—	2	1	10
Provost Corps	2	39	1	—	—	7	—	18	1	21
Intell. Corps	2	13	—	3	—	—	—	5	2	5
	305	4658	54	828	40	547	119	1754	132	2078

The figures given above for Wounded represent the actual number of wounded men *evacuated*. A further 570 wounded were left behind and are included in the total of Prisoners.

A study of the casualty analysis is interesting and reflects all too clearly the actual conditions on the various beaches.

Puys was a massacre. Except for three, every man who stepped ashore on this beach stayed there, either dead or a prisoner.

The three regiments landed at Dieppe lost over 400 in dead alone, and the figures for men of these units evacuated show that all efforts were directed to White Beach, where 345 were taken off as against only 52 from Red Beach. Apart from these formations, the worst hit were the Tank Regiment and the Royal Canadian Engineers, both of whom left behind almost half their embarked strength.

At Pourville the Cameron Highlanders and the South Saskatchewan Regiment suffered almost exactly the same proportion of total casualties, i.e. two-thirds of the embarked strength, although here a large number of wounded was brought back.

No detailed analysis of losses to the British Commandos is available, but total figures are as follows:

Commando Group No. 3	13 Officers and 113 Other Ranks
Commando Group No. 4	5 Officers and 40 Other Ranks
Royal Marine Commando	7 Officers and 93 Other Ranks

killed, wounded and prisoners.

Select Bibilography

Bernard Fergusson: *The Watery Maze* (Collins, London, 1961).

Derek Mills-Roberts: *Clash by Night* (William Kimber, London, 1957).

R. W. Queen-Hughes: *Whatever Men Dare*. The Regimental History of the Cameron Highlanders of Canada (Bulman, Winnipeg, 1960).

Colonel Stacey: *Six Years of War*, 1939–45. The official Canadian History (The Queen's Printer, Ottawa, 1948).

Peter Young: *Storm from the Sea* (William Kimber, London, 1959).

REIGN OF HELL BY SVEN HASSEL

Burning, looting, raping, murdering, Hitler's Penal Regiments advanced on the centre of Warsaw leaving in their wake a bloody trail of death and destruction. They killed indiscriminately. Pole or German; young or old; man, woman, child – anyone who crossed their path was eliminated. For Himmler had sworn that Warsaw would be razed to the ground – if it took every member of the German army to do it! And against the Fuhrer's expendable battalions, for whom life had no meaning, the battle for Warsaw became an inferno – an endless reign of hell . . .

0 552 09178 2   40p

SS GENERAL BY SVEN HASSEL

The 27th Panzers in Hitler's Penal Regiment had fought through the winter in the hell-hole that was Stalingrad. Now there were few survivors from the last massive Russian attack. Weary and nauseated by the horrors they'd seen on the Russian front, they crawled into a bunker near the banks of the Volga. Hunger, they had discovered, was more demoralizing than fear of defeat. Then the brutal SS general arrived . . .

0 552 08874 9   40p

THE SAVAGE MOUNTAIN BY WILLI HEINRICH

Three German soldiers hole up in a tiny Czech village, the suspected headquarters of the partisans. They pretend to be deserters – but each one has his own pattern for survival, each one lives in the constant awareness that some time will come the crushing degradation of complete physical and moral defeat, the frightful havoc of a once-powerful army crushed and battered into the mud – and the terrible moment that would surely come, the time to live – or the time to die . . .

552 09485 4   40p

THE WILLING FLESH BY WILLI HEINRICH

Sergeant Steiner was in command of ten men – survivors of a German rearguard trapped fifty miles behind the Russian lines. Their path to freedom led straight through the whole Russian army, together with all the murderous hazards of war – hunger, exhaustion, treachery, death. In the end, Steiner and his men were no longer fighting for Fuhrer or Fatherland, but for their naked, desperate lives . . .

The savage novel of the death throes of the German Wehrmacht.

552 09484 6   40p

SLAVES OF THE SON OF HEAVEN

BY R. H. WHITECROSS

In the burning, fever-ridden jungles of Burma, the Australian prisoners slaved on the dreaded Burma-Thailand railway – the railroad of death ...

Here, Japanese guns, bayonets and boots smashed at human pride and endurance – but until death came, they struggled on, through adversities beyond all human conception ...

0 552 09367 X   35P

THREE CAME HOME BY AGNES KEITH

After four years of Japanese occupation, the Allies regained Borneo, and the disease-ridden, emaciated inmates of Kuching prison-camp were free.

This is the true story of the horror and violence of life in that prison-camp. It is also the story of the women who had to fight a more vicious war than on any front, a war against starvation, exhaustion, disease, filth and the cruelty of the 'Nips' in Colonel Suga's 'Ideal Internment Camp'.

0 552 09368 8   35P

FLAME THROWER BY ANDREW WILSON

This is the first book to describe the activities of a Crocodile – one of the venomous flame-throwing Churchills – of which there were only fifty in the entire Allied Armies.

Towing armoured trailers full of liquid fire which would be pumped out of the tank's turret, a Crocodile could reduce a fortified house to a raging inferno in a matter of seconds, or the enemy trenches to a charred rubble . . .

FLAME THROWER is a fascinating account of the ordeals and triumphs of a man wielding one of these formidable, even horrifying weapons of war as they blazed their way across France to the Rhine.

0 552 09382 3   35p

THE LONG DAY'S DYING BY ALAN WHITE

Somewhere in Europe, in the middle of the second world war, three men from a commando unit have been detailed to watch a hill. They are fighting their own war, not only against a professional enemy, but against fatigue, physical pain, and a sense of having been abandoned. They are all specialists: trained to jump by parachute, to handle a knife or a piano wire – trained to kill.

To each of them the war is something different; their reasons for volunteering for this dangerous work highly individual. What those reasons are becomes apparent after the arrival of Helmut starts the long day on its inexorable path of dying.

0 552 09307 6   30p

THE SECRETS OF D-DAY BY GILLES PERRAULT

Here is the gigantic, minute-by-minute account of the duel between the German espionage services and Allied counter intelligence – a duel that resulted in the German High Command not believing in D-Day – when the troops were actually fighting on the Normandy beaches.

'These are themes which have naturally been touched on in other accounts but never so fully. They are sparkingly presented.' – *Times Literary Supplement*

552 09510 8   40p

YELLOW PERIL BY GILBERT HACKFORTH-JONES

Noël Coward's lines – (with acknowledgments) –

> It's such a surprise when the British own the earth
> They give rise to such hilarity and mirth

– are the inspiration behind Gilbert Hackforth-Jones's nostalgic picture of naval life in North China in the latter part of the 1920's.
   In that far-flung outpost of the Empire, on which at that period of history the sun never set, the naval warriors, on whose hands peacetime hung heavily, were busily occupying their minds and bodies in delight of simple things such as sport and womenfolk – until the menace of the Yellow Peril interceded in twenty-four hours of tragi-comedy.

0 552 09259 2   35p

A SELECTED LIST OF WAR
BOOKS THAT APPEAR IN CORGI

All these books are available at your bookshop or newsagent: or can be ordered direct from the publisher. Just tick the titles you want and fill in the form below.

CORGI BOOKS, Cash Sales Department, P.O. Box 11, Falmouth, Cornwall.

Please send cheque or postal order. No currency, and allow 10p per book to cover the cost of postage and packing (plus 5p each for additional copies).

NAME (*Block letters*) ....

ADDRESS ....

(AUG 74) ....

While every effort is made to keep prices low, it is sometimes necessary to increase prices at short notice. Corgi Books reserve the right to show new retail prices on covers which may differ from those previously advertised in the text or elsewhere.